Hookahs Horses

The Yard

Book One

Written and Illustrated
By

A.E. Hook

authorHOUSE®

AuthorHouse™
1663 Liberty Drive
Bloomington, IN 47403
www.authorhouse.com
Phone: 1-800-839-8640

This is a part fact part fiction story/collection of stories which are written for the true horse owner by a horse owner. This story is full of humour and will have you wanting more. It is based on thirty years experience and is centered on a few owners and their horses depicting the day to day events of owning a horse in an English 'Do It Yourself' yard.

All characters are fictional and any resemblance to living or dead is purely coincidental. However Dafydd and Al are based on the author and her horse.

Published by AuthorHouse   06/05/2012

ISBN: 978-1-4685-0423-1 (sc)
ISBN: 978-1-4685-0424-8 (e)

Any people depicted in stock imagery provided by Thinkstock are models, and such images are being used for illustrative purposes only.
Certain stock imagery © Thinkstock.

This book is printed on acid-free paper.

I'm Mistabit and I ask that you please don't copy, but buy The Yard. My mistress and I need to eat and I do like my carrots.

Hi, I am Mistabit, Misty for short. I am a six year old black Welsh Cob (with one white hind foot: hence my name) and I am owned by Alison. In real life I arrived at Al's yard when I was eighteen months old. I knew Dafydd and learnt a few things from him, much to Al's annoyance plus I also have a few little habits of my own, so far I have destroyed three feed buckets, two head-collars and one bridle, I haven't quite got the knack of throwing her off yet as it takes too much effort so I just do everything she asks of me slowly; which drives her mad and wears her out! There is another horse here called Tucker, he is a twenty-eight year old Thoroughbred and retired but I keep him fit by chasing him round the field occasionally; he can still go for an old chap. There is also an empty stable that was Dafydd's, sadly he is no longer with us, I am distantly related to him and I feature in the next book so spread the word about 'The Yard' so that book two and book three can be published.

This book is dedicated to my wonderful, intelligent Welsh Cob Dafydd who was my inspiration in the creation of Hookahs Horses cartoons and The Yard.

He was born on May 1st 1983 and passed away on July 14th 2011

He was put to sleep by injection and died peacefully at home with me, a gentleman to the end. We were together for 27 remarkable years.

CONTENTS

CHAPTER ONE

THE NEW ARRIVAL

'Who's the new livery coming in Trace?' Alison asked.

'It's a lad called Robert, he's got a cob type and he says it's a shire cross called Lennie' Trace offered Al a sweet trying to hold the bag so Al could only get one.

'Should be fun!' Al grinned as she took a handful, Trace just wasn't quick enough.

The yard is a small do-it-yourself yard mainly inhabited by young adults and some children who on the whole get on well together. There are eight stables with a hay barn and saddle room and a floodlit sand school. The owner is hardly ever seen, even when there are fencing and building repairs to be done; as a result the liveries do the repairs as best they can with the tools and materials that they have available.

Alison and Tracy are friends and have been on the yard for some time so they run the yard between them. Alison owns a 14.2hh Welsh Cob called Dafydd who she has owned since he was nine months old and Tracy has a 14.2hh 'thoroughbred type' called Lyric who can accelerate faster then anything else on four legs.

Midge is a black Shetland who like every Shetland goes where she pleases, when she pleases, she helps herself to others feed, goes into any stable that is open and escapes by crawling under the fencing. Midge is owned by the yard owner, who left her on the yard one day; as a result everyone chips in for her feed and bedding. Lucy rides Midge and looks after her when she can; she lives locally and loves horses but cannot afford one of her own so she has adopted Midge.

Primrose is a chestnut Arab who is owned by Sarah. Primrose is the best thing on the planet; no other horse can do so much or looks as pretty as Primrose this is according to Sarah. Everyone accepts Sarah's perception of her horse although not everyone agrees.

Dancer is a Thoroughbred who was bred to flat race but didn't make it, so Jill bought him at auction two years ago and is only now just managing to get him to stop when she asks and not when he wants to. She has tried every bit in existence; every gadget devised but in the end only schooling and lunging has had any effect.

George is a palomino with unknown history; Mike has owned him for two months after he saw him at a horse market tied to a lorry that was bound for the meat factory. Mike could not leave him there and so persuaded his dad to buy him for thirty pounds; he named him George after his favourite singer George Michael.

'He's here Trace.'

A lorry pulled up in the car park and reversed up to the gate; a good looking chap got out and unbolted the ramp lowering it to the floor.

'Hey Trace do you think that is Robert, if so he's mine.'

'Behave yourself; besides he's too old for you, he's mine.'

Inside the lorry was a young lad holding onto a very large horse.

'Could you open the gate please and stand to one side?' The lad asked.

Trace opened the gate to the yard and was almost thrown to one side as the horse trotted by with the lad being dragged behind him.

'Al, Al, where are you?'

Al was having a chat with the chap who unbolted the horsebox ramp.

'What Trace can't you see I'm busy?'

'Well if you can manage to tear yourself away from your imaginary love life I think the lad could do with some help.'

'No thanks I'm fine, Lennie gets a little over excited when he goes out in the box, my name is Robert.'

'So who is the chap with the horsebox?'

'That's my older brother John.'

'Hey you don't have another older, older brother for Trace do you!' Al grinned.

Lennie was fed up waiting around and so started off again in the direction of the horses in the fields with Robert behind him trying to hang on. Al and Trace grabbed a lead rope each and launched themselves at Lennie's head-collar one either side. Once they had clipped on they both pulled back and Lennie stopped, which startled Lennie, as he had never been stopped before. Al and Trace then guided him towards his stable, Lennie co-operated to begin with then realised new tactics were needed, so he stopped and refused to move.

'Robert grab that broom and smack him across the backside with it, otherwise we will be standing here all day.'

Robert picked up the broom and waved it behind Lennie who took no notice.

'No hit him with it.' Trace yelled.

Robert smacked Lennie who moved forward initially in his desired direction but Al and Trace soon redirected him to his stable. Once in, his travel clothes were removed and he was left to settle in.

'It's not often anyone can persuade him to do things, you generally just have to hope he co-operates.' Robert said.

'I'm amazed that you're still alive Robert! Well that won't work here he will have to do as he is told as he is too big with too small a brain to do as he pleases, give him a feed and a wormer and he can go out in the small paddock tomorrow.'

Lennie was not amused at being put in a stable, as he was use to being out. Lennie stood with his head over the door snorting with disgust and neighing to any horse that would listen; occasionally a good kick of the door got some attention although not the sort he was looking for! Eventually Al became fed up with the door bashing, as none of the stables had top doors she nailed a board across the door gap to prevent Lennie getting his head over the door and kicking it.

'Trace are you riding out or schooling?' Al enquired.

'Don't know, I thought I would hack out.'

'Alright I'll come too, Daff could do with a blast on the common.'

'Shall we wait for Gill?'

'What and end up riding for half an hour instead of two. No she won't be down until later anyway.'

Al and Trace tacked up Daff and Lyric in their best numnah's and boots, as they were 'going out in public'. Al was in her white and black and Trace was in blue with a hint of red on the numnah. Trace and Al also had their fluorescent tops on, as car drivers are so thick they can't see a horse let alone two unless something bright is worn and even then they try and squeeze past.

The roads from the yard are narrow and so Trace and Al rode in single file with Al in front and Trace behind as Lyric had previously been hit by a car and so became easily upset on the roads. Daff on the other hand didn't bother about anything; this is either because he's thick or too lazy to waste energy on messing about.

'Shall we go to the Mill; we can stop off at the café for a bite to eat?' Trace said hopefully.

'Why not it's a nice day, with a bit of luck it won't be too busy.'

'Al, we have a car behind better let him pass.'

Daff and Lyric moved over into a lay-by to allow the car to pass, as the road was narrow and they were only walking. Once the car passed they moved out only to have another car come up behind them this time with loud music, Lyric started to get upset as the car was right behind him.

'Al you had better trot on this idiot behind obviously has not read the Highway Code and he is right behind me.'

The girls trotted on but the car remained behind, he then started revving his engine and tooting his horn, with this Lyric started to canter, Trace tried to calm him without success. Al waved the car on so he could overtake but he just sat behind them deliberately trying to wind the horses up.

'Trace, go in front of me.'

Trace went in front which calmed Lyric a little; the driver used his horn again. Al was furious so she stopped Daff and turned him around.

'What the hell is your problem, are you incapable of overtaking. Do you only know how to use your horn, these are only dumb animals but they have more brain capacity then you do!' Al never minced her words.

'Get off the road I pay road tax and insurance you shouldn't be allowed to use the roads, especially when you can't control those horses, so get out my way or I will run you over.' Sneered the driver.

Al got out her mobile and rang the police; she gave them the car registration number as the driver sped off. Trace and Al continued with their ride trying not to allow the incident to ruin their day. They eventually reached the common, which caters for walkers as well as riders; people would walk on the common on a Sunday afternoon in particular with their children and dogs. Horse Riders loved the common early in the morning when there were no flies or walkers around, as dogs chasing horses was a common problem as well as walkers on the bridleways. The riders enjoyed the quietness of the wood with its winding tracks and surrounding wildlife all of which was becoming less due to housing developments and roads as well as golf courses.

At the other end of the common was an old flourmill that had been changed into a café and bar, unlike most places they had made provision for horses and their riders. Al and Trace got off and tied the horses up near the water trough while they went and got their tea and cakes. They sat down at a table that was near to the horses so that they could keep an eye on them. Daff took exception at not having a cake bought for him and so he swung his quarters round and lashed out at the table with both back legs catching the table, which resulted in the food and drink ending up on the floor.

'I suppose you think that's funny Daff?' Al scorned.

'I told you to buy him a bun you know what he is like.' Giggled Trace, who had seen what was going to happen and so grabbed her food and drink before the table went.

The café owner saw what happened and gave Al a free bun and a cup of tea as well as a bun for Daff and of course one for Lyric as well.

Once the girls had refuelled they mounted up and headed back home. Many tracks on the common had been specially laid as 'gallop tracks' for horses, they were very wide and surfaced with sand. Walkers had their own tracks which ran alongside the horse tracks.

'Watch out Al.' Trace yelled.

Too late Al had hit the track with a thud as Daff had swung round and fly kicked at a dog that had run up behind him, Daff then took full advantage of Al being separated from him and cantered off.

'Get after him Trace, I'm all right'

Al was furious; she picked herself up and dug the sand out from her jodhpurs and boots and other places!

'Are you all right dear?' The owner of the dog asked.

'Oh yes I'm fine, I love sitting on the wet ground while my horse bolts off due to your dog not being under control on a bridle track which I would like to point out is for horses not people and their unruly pets!' Al took a breath before she went purple.

With that Al walked off in the direction that Daff went.

'You all right Al?' Trace was dragging Daff behind her and Lyric.

'Yes, I see you managed to catch him.'

'He stopped at a fence which had horses on the other side, I guess he thought he was home, he hasn't hurt himself.'

'Thanks Trace, I guess that's three things in a row, so we should be able to get home without anything else happening.'

Al; being a bit short in the leg department, found a log and got back on, they all headed back home without further trouble.

Once back at the yard the girls untacked and finished laying their beds. Daff and Lyric were put in the sand school to have a roll before they were put to bed. Daff came in covered in wet, muddy, sand as he had rolled in the corner of the school, which did not drain properly.

'Looks like your going to be a while Al it's going to take some brushing to get that lot off.'

'I really hate him sometimes and I wanted to get away early as well, I'm sure he does this deliberately just to wind me up.'

Al eventually managed to scrape the sand off Daff and put him to bed, she checked all the lights were off; gates were locked and went home.

When the yard is quiet and free of humans the horses chat amongst themselves:

'You were really rotten to do that to your mistress today Daff' Lyric whinnied.

'What does she expect getting herself something to eat and not me, after I had done all the work carrying her across the common?'

'Well I can understand knocking the table over but you then went and chucked her on the floor.'

'Now that wasn't my fault I was trying to protect myself, it's not my fault she can't stay on.'

'But you didn't wait for her to get back on you took advantage and ran off and then my mistress and I had to go and get you which meant I had to do extra work.'

'Oh sorry about that Lill's. Anyway you started it all by mucking about on the road.'

'That's not fair you know I had that mishap with a car, I just can't cope with cars behind me, it's frightening.'

'Good job I'm around then isn't it?'

'Excuse me chaps, my name is Lennie I just moved in today.'

'Hi, I am Lyric and this is Dafydd, where have you come from.'

'I don't really know it was quite a long trip in the box. My master is very nice he allows me to do anything I want, but I'm not to keen on your mistresses they were rather rough with me when I arrived.'

'What do you expect dragging your master around the yard; I think you are in for a few surprises mate.' Daff snorted.

Daff had already decided that he wasn't keen on Lennie, as Daff liked to be the centre of attention when it came to misbehaviour!

CHAPTER TWO

IT'S SHOW TIME

There was a turn out rota on the yard as well as a rota for cleaning shelters and water tanks which did not always run according to plan as excuses were made and so it always resulted in a certain few; normally Trace and Al to do the chores. As the owner of the yard was never around Al had to collect the rent monthly and post it to the owner, this was also a chore as there was always one who was late or had forgotten their chequebook.

Saturdays were set aside for repairs and show preparation, as Sundays were show days. Trace and Al share a trailer, which Trace pulls with her Land Rover. Sarah has a horse-box which can carry two horses this often leads to the other horse owners fussing round Sarah to get a place in her box so that they could go to shows as well. Sarah loved this as she would get her stable mucked out and horse groomed for nothing. Trace and Al always knew when Sarah was going to a show as the others would start to pamper Sarah, when a show wasn't on Sarah got to do her own cleaning, fetching and carrying

Shows were always a popular topic on the yard, who had done what, what had been won and almost won! Tracey often competed in long distance rides and cross-country while Alison preferred show jumping and more latterly Dressage, Daff liked the Dressage as it was less exerting and he could show off. For years Al was unsuccessful when competing, she hardly ever won a rosette and so decided to do something about it and so she began lessons with an instructor who was recommended to her. A previous instructor had left Al wondering whether this new instructor would be any good as he was unable to help Alison achieve any rosettes. Alison was given riding school horses which were all above fifteen hands and hard work so she decided she would continue the lessons on Daff as that is what she had to work with. Initially Alison did not like the instructor, as she would sit in the corner puffing on one cigarette after another and yelling instructions, she yelled even louder when Al got it wrong. What was more infuriating was that it was always Al's fault; 'darling Dafydd' never put a foot wrong! Slowly the results showed Daff started to be placed and on a few occasions won preliminary Dressage competitions against Dressage type horses who had more often then not been purchased for the job.

'Trace are you going to the Langhorn show on Sunday?' Al enquired hopefully.

'I think so, looks like the whether is going to be nice and the ground should be good.'

'It would be a good starter for the Charston show in two weeks.'

'Have they got any Cross-Country on Al?'

'They have a small course as well as Show-Jumping and Dressage.'

'Is Sarah going on Sunday?'

'Of course she is, there is Arab in-hand showing, haven't you noticed Jill mucking Prim out?'

Sunday came, all week the girls had been putting the finishing touches to their horses and polishing off their display routines as well as practising their jumping techniques. Al did not have to plait Daff's mane as it had been hogged, Trace was plaiting Lyric and Sarah left hers natural. Jill was undecided, as this was the first show she was going to with Dancer it would also probably be the last by the time Dancer had finished with her!

The first hurdle was to get the horses loaded; Trace and Al predicted that there would be a problem loading Dancer next to Prim so they waited until these two were loaded before they loaded theirs.

'Right come on Jill let's get Dancer in first.' Al insisted.

'Would it not be better to put Prim in first?'

'No, Dancer will upset Prim lets sort him out first.'

Jill had put on Dancer's travelling boots and rug, she led him up the ramp and as predicted he stopped dead with one foot on the ramp.

'Just let him look and have a think Jill.' Trace advised.

Jill waited and waited and waited then Dancer walked straight up, Prim was an old hand at loading and so loaded without hesitation.

'Right Trace now they are sorted out let's get going.'

'Load Daff first Al as he can be a bit stubborn.'

Al put Daff's travelling boots and rug on and walked him up the trailer ramp where he stopped.

'Trace grab your lunge rein and put it behind him, I have one in the trailer.'

Al connected her lunge rein to Daff's head-collar and then put it round the breast bar, with gloves on she held onto the rein. Daff started to go backwards but Trace had the rein behind him and Al had 'locked' the rein off around the breast bar. Daff stepped forwards hoping to be released but Al just shortened the rein, Daff started to get annoyed but he couldn't go anywhere he ran forwards which is exactly what Al wanted, she released the rein and tied him up with a hay-net. Next was Lyric, he walked straight in with no problem at all.

At the show ground Sarah had already unloaded and was putting on her show clothes, she wore a red skirt and jacket with matching hat and show stick, and Jill was putting on hoof oil and grooming Prim. Daff and Lyric were unloaded; Daff made sure everyone knew he had arrived by yelling his head off. Once the horses were settled the girls entered their classes and got their numbers as well at stopping off at the refreshment stall for a snack.

'Don't let Daff see you eating that burger you know what he is like.'

'Too late he's already spotted me.'

Daff loved bread and a cup of tea with sugar if he could get it, he had spotted Al and so started to whinny and scrape the ground as well as rearing and tossing his head.

'You will have to give him some or he will make you pay later.'

'All right here you are Daff, I had better get a rosette today or that is the last piece of bread you will taste.'

Once Al and Trace had finished their snack they started to tack the boys up, they had both entered the best rider class and the 2'6" show jumping, Best Rider was first.

'Would all competitors for the Best Rider class go to ring Three and Arab in Hand to ring four, thank you'

Jill had also entered the Best Rider class along with seven other competitors. Al and Trace watched the competition as they went round they also kept an eye on the judge so that they could look their best when she was looking at them. The judge called them into the centre and asked each rider in turn to do their display. First to go was Jill, Dancer started off well but gradually became faster and faster. Jill was really struggling to get him back to a trot from canter, Dancer then stopped, reared and then he tried to bolt. Inevitably the judge asked Jill to stop and leave the arena, as she was a danger to the other horses, this became evident when Dancer ploughed into the end horse causing all the horses to run for it!

Lyric's turn came and he, as usual, did a lovely display, lengthened strides a flying change, he could not be faulted. Then it was Daff's turn, Al had practised all week her display routine but that all went out the window when Daff started by shaking his head from side to side, this was a clear indication that he was not going to co-operate. His strides became shorter he started to bunch up, the bomb was about to explode! Al quietly swore at him out of the judges hearing range, she tightened her grip hoping this would make Daff think twice about his behaviour, Daff knew he was going to be in big trouble if he bucked and bolted but he didn't care. Al's display was going well she had almost finished when Daff could not contain himself any longer, he lunged forward and stuck his head between his legs pulling Al out of the saddle in the process. He then leapt forward and bucked but Al regained her seat, she pulled as hard as she could on the reins to get control of Daff's head. Daff leaned heavily on the bit hoping to wear Al out, but Al was not having any of it. The display was ruined but she could not let Daff win, she squeezed with both legs pushing Daff on, at the same time collecting Daff up, she eventually won, much to Daff's disgust. Al halted and saluted the judge and went back to her place. Once all the displays were done the competitors moved off and the judge called the horses in order of their place, Lyric came in second and Daff in seventh, at least he wasn't last. The judge said that Daff was a nice chap and that Al had done well to stay on him and get him under control.

Al dumped Daff back at the trailer and went to watch Sarah in her class. There were six in the class and of course Sarah stuck out due to her red outfit, Prim did look quite good and stood a chance of winning. The Arabs were lined up and each in turn was walked away from the judge and trotted back. Jill and Trace joined Al at the ring; Trace had her 2nd place rosette hooked through her buttonhole.

'Oh did you win a rosette Trace I would not have known if you had not worn it so openly.'

'It's not my fault Daff was difficult, besides that, if you've got it, flaunt it.'

'I hope your exhaust pipe rots and falls off Trace, you wait till the show-jumping class.'

'If it does you will have to find someone else to take you to shows, and you think you are going to have a chance against Lyric and me in the show-jumping, in your dreams.'

'Oi you two grow up and shut up.' Jill was trying to watch the Arabs.

Sarah was called out with Primrose, she walked away from the Judge and then trotted back, all was going well until Prim's flowing elevated trot caught Sarah's long, flowing skirt, which resulted in it wrapping around Sarah's ankles and Sarah nose diving to the ground with her backside in full view! Sarah quickly picked herself up along with her skirt and continued her display. The judge could barely keep a straight face when Sarah returned to salute him. Sarah's face was as red as her skirt; it was undecided as to whether this was due to embarrassment, anger or physical effort. Jill, Trace and Al started to laugh and had to move away from the ring so Sarah could not see them. Sarah was placed third even though she fell over as it was judged on the horse not the owner.

Al, Trace and Jill returned to the trailer and pretended that they did not see Sarah's display.

'Hi, Sarah how did you do?' Al asked innocently.

'Did you not watch the class?'

'No we were all in Best Rider.' Replied all three together.

'Oh, well it was quite a large class and there were some very nice Arabs in there so we only managed a third.'

'What happened to your skirt Sarah?' Trace asked with a straight face.

'Oh dear must have caught it somewhere.'

'Would all competitors for the 2'6"
jumping go to ring two, thank you'

'Come on Trace that's us, are you jumping Jill?'

'No I have had enough for one day.'

Trace and Al changed some of their tack and went to the jump arena. There were over twenty competitors Trace went first and cleared all the jumps at her usual speed of 100mph. Al went next, Daff was in a better mood and forward going, he cleared the first jump as it was towards the entrance he then tried to go through the entrance but Al was ready for him and so drove him round the corner to the second jump. Daff tried to back off the third jump, but Al was not having any of it she was determined to go clear which she did. At the end of the first round twelve horses went clear, now for the jump off. Trace was first again and although she was fast she had two poles down.

'Bad luck Trace, shame about those two poles.'

Al was relieved, as she had no chance of beating Lyric for speed, Al also knew that Daff spent more time in the air then covering the ground. Al's turn came she took Daff up the back of the arena and circled him to get him moving forward, the buzzer went Al pushed Daff on and he jumped the first one clear. Al had to take some tricky short cuts to stand any chance of winning; she knew if Daff jumped he would not knock anything down. The round finished quickly and Daff was clear but he was not fast enough and so came in third out of twelve, which was not bad considering his antics in the Best Rider class.

'Not bad Al, a few more seconds faster and you could have had a blue rosette like me.' Trace grinned.

'All right Trace, at least I got through the jump off and won a rosette.'

'Lyric would have won if he had not caught his foot in a pot hole.'

'Strange how two separate jumps had potholes, very unlucky that.'

'Come on I have had enough for one day let's go home.'

Sarah had already left with Jill.

'Trace put Lyric in first see if Daff would go in second without a fight.'

Trace loaded Lyric and then Daff was taken to the trailer, he, as usual stopped on the ramp but Al was ready with the rein after a little fight Daff loaded.

'I don't know why you bother mate, you come in eventually, I guess you just want to protest don't you!' Daff tossed his head and lunged at his hay net in disgust.

The girls drove back to the yard and unloaded the horses allowing them to spend the rest of the day in the field while they cleaned out the trailer and car. Sarah had put Prim in the field and left Jill to clean out the horsebox.

'Why don't you get your own trailer Jill instead of clearing up after Sarah?' Al asked.

'I am saving up for a trailer until then I have to be nice to her.'

'What are you going to do about Dancer, you can't keep on making excuses for him he's going to injure himself, you or someone soon.'

'I know, I will have to send him away to be retrained if he doesn't start responding soon, or get an instructor.'

'Get an instructor; both you and him need to be taught together.'

'Whoa, Lennie, stop . . . help.'

Lennie had barged through the gate and was dragging Robert across the yard.

'Robert you are really going to have to get control of that horse, Trace give us hand.'

Trace and Al once again grabbed lead ropes and attached themselves to either side of Lennie's head-collar and guided him to his stable, much to Lennie's disgust.

As the sun set the horses were put away and the owners went home.

'Lennie you are going to get into a lot of trouble if you keep dragging your master around.'

'I was bored in that tiny paddock, how did you do today?'

'I didn't manage to get my mistress off but she didn't win much, so it was a fairly successful day.' Daff whinnied with delight.

'At least I try for my mistress Daff, you are nothing but a hooligan. She feeds you and looks after you and all you do is embarrass her and play the fool.'

'Ooh, and who rocked your boat Lyric, Gods gift to horses. You think you are so brilliant at least I can get over a jump without taking it with me!'

'My foot slipped in a hole, so I lost my concentration.'

'What at two jumps?'

CHAPTER THREE

BAD MANNERS

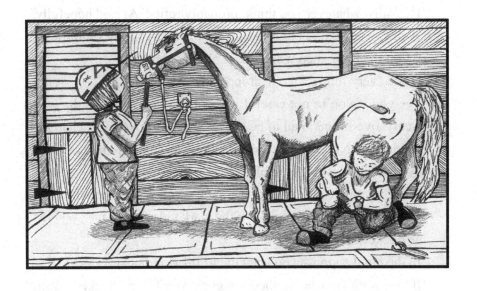

'What time is he due Trace?'

'He should be here at ten.'

'Are you having a full set or refits?'

'Probably refits he hasn't done much roadwork.'

Wally the farrier was due to shoe Daff, Dancer and Lyric, he had been shoeing Daff since he was four years old and was use to Daff's rocking horse antics. Wally arrived and got out his anvil and tools and lit his mobile furnace. Wally was a big burly chap with side-burns who began his shoeing career in the army at least thirty years ago.

'Hi ya girls, what we having today then?'

'Hi Wally, whatever you think, probably refits!' Al said hopefully.

'Well if you wanted racing plates why didn't you say so, these are so thin the scrap man will be poor.' Wally chuckled.

'Ha-ha, very funny anyone dropped dead lately?'

'Yes you if you're not careful. One of my oldest clients, he were twenty-five I think, had to be shot yesterday. Lovely old chap just couldn't keep weight on.' Wally had a slight northern accent and loved to rib Al when he could.

'I take it you mean a horse and not the owner?' Al smirked.

'Oh, we are awake and quick off the mark today aren't we? Where's me bucket of water then?'

'In the tap, I suppose you want me to fill your bucket?'

'If you want your horse shod I suggest you fill me bucket.' Wally winked.

This banter continued until Wally had finished, each horse took about forty-five minutes to shoe. Wally finished Daff and started on Dancer. Dancer lived up to his name he could not stand still for five minutes.

'I'm glad I don't have too many horses like you mate.' Wally cursed.

Dancer kept on pulling his foot away from Wally. Eventually Wally started to nail the shoes on then Wally winced and cursed loudly as

Dancer pulled his foot away and a protruding nail ripped into the side of Wally's hand. The blood started to drip onto the ground, Al grabbed her medical kit and helped Wally clean the wound and dress it.

'That horse is going to have to find some manners or it's going to have to find a new farrier.'

'I don't blame you Wally, he is has no manners and even less discipline, Jill is thinking about sending him away'

'What to the knackerman, good idea.'

'No to be re-schooled, although you might be right Wally!'

'You all right to finish off?'

'Yes I'll live, but he won't if he keeps on mucking about.'

'I will hold him you carry on.'

Al got a twitch and secured it on Dancer's nose slowly he relaxed and Wally finished shoeing him without further problems.

'That twitch worked well with him, remember to do that in future.'

Wally did Lyric next, whom as with everything was perfect. Wally finished up and was paid, fortunately he didn't have anymore horses that day to shoe as he started at seven in the morning.

'We are going to have to sort Dancer out Trace, Jill is not firm enough with him and it's not going to be long before someone gets seriously hurt.

'Your are right Al, let's get him tacked up and start schooling him.'

Al put Dancers' saddle and bridle on and then attached a lunge line, Trace got on and Al started to lunge him. Eventually Trace took over the commands and Al remained as back up in case Dancer started to bolt. Initially Dancer started well then he became faster and refused to stop. Trace pulled as hard as she could with little effect so Al gradually pulled on the lunge rein to slow Dancer and to pull him into a tighter circle. Dancer kept on going right to the last minute and then he stopped and reared. Trace remained in her seat and Al pulled down on the rein to keep him on the ground.

'He has no brakes and refuses to obey any leg commands; maybe we should change his bit?'

'Why don't we try a draw-rein then he can fight against himself and he won't be able to rear.'

Al got her draw-rein and put it on Dancer. Trace gradually shortened the rein until Dancer could feel it, Dancer walked very slowly, then trotted slowly and then he stopped and tried to rear, which failed completely because he could not get his head up. Dancer backed up and refused to walk forward, Trace released the draw-rein slightly with this Dancer went forward, once he realised he was free he bolted. Trace shortened the draw-rein again and was gradually able to stop Dancer. This continued for some time, eventually Dancer accepted the draw-rein and began to work quite well in it once he settled down the girls stopped, untacked him and turned him out.

'Well that was quite successful wasn't it Trace?'

'I will let you know tomorrow, that is if I am able to get out of bed and walk!'

'If only we could get Jill to do the same it would not be long before he had some manners.'

'Jill is not capable of doing that with him; she should have bought an old school horse not a lunatic like that.'

'Well she has him now and if he can't be put right he will end up with the knackerman.'

The girls finished off their mucking out.

'Al, the feed delivery is here.'

'I will be there in a minute get him to put it in the feed room will you Trace?'

'Ok are we paying now or later?'

'Get the receipt and I will pay later.'

Al ordered the feed on a monthly basis; it was delivered free of charge and then divided up amongst the owners after they had paid for it. Al had in the past given it to the owners and then waited ages to be paid so now the feed is not given out until it is paid for.

'Al have you seen Midge I thought she was in middle field with the others but I cannot see her!'

'I bet she has escaped into Mrs Brown's garden again, she has a liking for her prize roses, but she couldn't have because I boarded up her hole in the fence.'

The girls went and checked middle field and Mrs Brown's garden but Midge was no where to be seen. They returned to the yard to see if Midge had been shut in a stable by mistake.

'I expect it will not be long before someone finds her and brings her back'

'Robert have you seen Midge the black Shetland?'

'I saw her over by the tack room a little while ago.'

'If you see her on the yard in future Robert grab her and put her back in the field don't just let her wander around.'

'Al guess what?'

'What Trace, I'm not in the mood for games?'

'You know that feed we have just had delivered, well Midge rather likes the mix and the chaff!'

'Your joking, it's just been delivered how the devil did she know?'

'She probably read the writing on the delivery lorry!' Trace quipped.

Al ran to the feed room to find three sacks of mix and one bag of herbal chaff ripped open and spilling onto the floor. Midge was standing in the middle of it munching away to her hearts content. The girls grabbed her and dragged her away from her late lunch to the field, making certain they bolted the feed room door shut behind them.

'Whose feed was it that Midge got Al?'

'The herbal chaff and a mix was Sarah's and the other two mixes were Jill's.'

'Jill is feeding mix to Dancer?'

'Yes, I have told her but she thinks he needs the energy as he young and is being worked.'

'No wonder he is popping out of his skull all the time. She only rides him two or three times a week if that!'

'I know, but what can you do, it is her horse.'

'Order her a non-heating mix or pasture nuts and say they were out of mix.'

'That's not a bad idea; I'll do that next time. Good thinking Trace.'

'We had better try and salvage what is left of the feed and prevent any rats having a feast as well as Midge.'

The girls swept up the spilt feed and taped up the bags where midge had chewed open the paper sacks. Trace and Al put their feed in the metal feed bins, which prevented the rats from eating it. The rat population was very low due to the surrounding houses having several cats who visited the yard on a regular basis for a bit of sport. Most of the rats that were present came to the yard from the houses, which had compost heaps so it was only right that their cats should sort the rats out.

Just as the girls had finished a loud crack of wood was heard and then the clanging of hooves, Al and Trace peered round the door to find all the horses on the yard.

'Quick Trace make sure the gates are closed and grab some head-collars. Robert get some head-collars and help round the horses up.'

While Trace and Robert secured the horses Al went to see what had given way to allow the horses onto the yard. Most of the fencing was post and rail some rails had barbed wire but not all. Al saw straight away what had given, the gate was smashed in several places, Al started to clear the broken timbers, the hinges were still in one piece although a little buckled and one of the posts was broken completely.

'Oh dear he's done it again!' Robert sighed as he released a horse back into the adjoining field.

'What, you mean this is a little habit of Lennie's . . . smashing gates, I don't remember you mentioning that when you asked to come here!'

'He hasn't done it for a long time; mind you that could be because the last place had metal gates on metal posts.'

'Well Robert you are about to learn how to make a gate, your horse broke it you can help to repair it!'

'I have a dentist's appointment in two hours.'

'Good, that gives you just enough time to dig out that broken post and put in a new one while I find some new timbers to make a gate with, tools are in the shed over there.'

Robert thought it best not to refuse or to make any further excuses he went and got a spade and began to dig the post out. Al found a replacement post but didn't have many screws or gate timbers; this meant she had to salvage what she could from the broken gate.

'Why don't you concrete the posts in?' Robert asked.

'Because when it snaps at ground level you will not only have to dig the post out but the concrete as well.'

'Oh, seems sensible. Why don't you purchase a new gate instead of making one?'

'Robert, I would like nothing more then to buy a gate, do you really think that I want to spend my spare time making gates for this place, think again.'

'No need to snap I only asked a simple question!'

'This is not the time to be asking questions.'

'Need a hand Al?' Trace enquired.

'Yes please, could you take the hinges off and straighten them out while I make the gate.'

'Will do, shall I make some tea first?'

'Let's have some after we have done this gate otherwise we will lose the light.'

Trace took the hinges off and straightened them with a hammer and brick and Robert put the new post in. Al's job was made easier by having an electric screwdriver and drill, it was not long before a new gate was made and hung, this time Al stapled on barbed wire to prevent Lennie from demolishing it.

'Hi girls had a nice day?'

'Oh smashing thanks Jill, we have captured Midge, salvaged the feed, repaired the gate and rounded up escaped horses. In addition to that, prevented the farrier from terminating your horse. So yes we have had a great day!'

'What has Wally done to my horse?'

'It's not a case of what Wally has done to Dancer but what Dancer has done to Wally. The idiot would not stand still and as a result ripped Wally's hand open on a nail.'

'Is Dancer all right?'

'Dancer is fine, however if he does not find some manners soon Wally will refuse to shoe him. Trace and I had a little word with Dancer.'

'What do you mean?'

Trace and Al explained to Jill what they had done; Jill was not happy that Dancer had been ridden so firmly but in her heart knew that Trace and Al were right. Sarah arrived to find out that Midge had sampled her feed, this wound her up a little but she exploded when she found out that Primrose might have been injured on the broken gate. She got Prim in and checked every inch demanding that either Lennie was put in another field or Prim was. Al and Trace refused, as the fields had to be rested, anyway horses need to be with horses. The girls got their stables ready and brought the horses in checking them all to make

---

sure no one had injured themselves on the broken gate; apart from a few scratches all the horses were fine.

'That was a bit of fun today Lennie.' George quipped.

'That's nothing you should see what I do in the show ring.'

'Oi Midge, if you eat my feed again you won't see tomorrow.' Dancer Snorted.

'Dancer you don't need any feed, the way you behave you should be locked up permanently.' Daff yelled.

All the horses whinnied and neighed in agreement.

'You were absolutely awful to Wally and he's such a nice man, mind you at least our mistresses sorted you out.'

'You think your mistresses had any affect on me, think again. Next time I will be ready.' Dancer snorted defiantly.

'You harm my mistress mate and I will make your life a misery in the field.' Daff advised.

'Oh so it's all right for you Daff to defy her and throw her off but not me?'

'She's my mistress and it's my right to throw her off not yours, so you have been warned.'

'And that goes for me too.' Lyric neighed.

CHAPTER FOUR

GREEDY GEORGE

'Tracey would you have a look at George he doesn't seem himself?' Mike asked.

'Sure I will Mike where is he?'

'He is in his stable, I only put on one rug last night but he is sweating and refuses to get up.'

Trace went to George's stable to find him lying down and groaning there were very few droppings and he refused to eat his breakfast.

'Who is your vet Mike?'

'I don't have one, why is George sick?'

'Yes Mike he is very ill and we need to get a vet to him now, I will call my vet.'

Trace got out her mobile and telephoned her vet, he agreed to come as soon as he finished with the client he was with.

'Mike have you fed him anything different, did he seem all right yesterday?'

'I fed him his usual feed, he seemed a little quiet and he was not that bothered about his feed although he did eventually eat it.'

'We can't do anything until the vet gets here we had better check the field.'

'What do you think is wrong Trace?'

'I think it is colic Mike.'

'Is that serious, he's not going to die is he?'

'We have to find the cause then we will have some idea as to what caused the colic. Look for anything that is not normally in the field, any rubbish or food, things like that.'

'He's going to be all right isn't he?'

'I hope so, come on lets check the field.'

Trace and Mike split up and walked round the field, some of the horses were already out and had gathered in the far corner of the field, they seemed to be very interested in something. Trace ran over to find them eating grass cuttings, which someone had thrown over the fence. Trace frightened the horses away and began to throw the cuttings back over the fence; they weren't just recent cuttings it was as though a whole compost heap had been thrown over.

'Mike give me a hand to chuck these grass cuttings back over the fence.'

'Is this what made George ill?'

'Probably, some people think that horses can eat cuttings but they can't.'

'Why aren't any of the others sick?'

'Some horses can tolerate things better then others; George may have eaten more.'

'Trace it looks like the vet is here.'

Trace and Mike ran back to the yard and spoke with the vet. The vet examined George and gave him a pain killing injection and other injections that would help him. It was colic, fortunately it was probably due to eating the grass cuttings and not a result of a twisted gut or impacted food as the vet could still hear some sounds from George's belly. The vet said that George should be kept in and given bran mashes, keep him warm and don't walk him or allow him to roll; if George became worse then they were to call him immediately.

'Hey Trace what was vet Simons doing here?' Al enquired.

'George has colic as a result of grass clippings being chucked in the field.'

'How many times do we have to tell people, is he going to be all right.'

'Simons thinks so, we have to keep him warm, no exercise and no rolling.'

'We had better put some straw bales behind him to stop him rolling.'

Al went to get some bales while Trace helped Mike muck out and make a bran mash. Mike's dad arrived to take him to school but Mike refused to go, he wanted to remain with George.

'Oh please dad, I can't leave George he's very ill, please let me stay off school just for today.'

'I think you should let Mike stay, I will be here all day and so will be around if anything happens.' Al said.

'All right just for today, I don't suppose you will do any work worrying about him.'

Mike left George's door open so he could see out as he refused to get up, Al placed a bale behind George so he could not roll and possibly make his colic worse. Al and Trace then went to the house from where the clippings had been thrown over. Al rang the door bell, the door opened.

'Yes can I help you?' A middle-aged lady asked.

'Hi, we have horses on the land behind you and we have just had to call a vet out as a result of one of the horses eating the grass cuttings that have been thrown over your fence.'

'Oh I am sorry my husband was clearing the bottom of the garden yesterday and some of the horses seemed to like the cuttings so he gave them to them.'

'Horses aren't like rabbits or cattle they can't eat salad stuff or grass cuttings let alone rotten ones, please don't, throw anything over the fence in future!'

'All right I will tell my husband, is the horse going to be ok?'

'We don't know.'

Al and Trace left before Al said something she shouldn't.

'How can people be so stupid? It's a good job you spoke to her Trace or I would have.'

'Yes I know Al, you have to remember that she doesn't have a horse so would not know that cuttings are not to be given to horses, what we should do is send her the vet bill she would not do it again then.'

'Even if they could eat grass cuttings that still does not give them the right to chuck their rubbish over the fence on to someone else's land, particularly when livestock are present.'

Al and Trace returned to the yard and inspected the fields more closely to ensure no other rubbish was present; they took an empty wheel barrow and returned with several glass bottles, ten drinks cans, four plastic bags, a dozen or more crisp bags and other potential lethal objects.

Some of the horses were quietly standing by the gate, which was not usual, as they would normally be grazing.

'It's strange isn't it Al, it's as though they are concerned about George.'

'More likely when the next feed is due. Mind you they are rather quiet even Lennie is motionless we had better hope no one else becomes ill.'

'Let's check on George.'

Trace and Al went to George's stable to find Mike had borrowed some rugs and was sitting on them in the stable with George. Mike had some schoolbooks with him and was doing some homework, which he should have completed the night before! Mike began to read a story to George from his English lesson unaware that Trace and Al were present; Trace and Al left Mike and started to muck out and tidy the yard.

Lunchtime came and Mike was still with George only leaving him to go to the toilet, Al and Trace went to the chip shop and got some lunch for themselves and Mike they also bought some tea, sugar and milk as supplies were running low.

'Mike we bought you some lunch come and get it.'

'Thanks, I'm starving. I think George is getting better he had a couple of mouthfuls of bran.'

'That's good Mike, are you not eating with us?'

'No, I will sit with George.'

Mike took his chips and a cup of tea and went back to George's stable.

'I hope George pulls through Trace, he's not had the best of times, and it would be tragic if he died just when he had found a loving owner.'

'Mike will be inconsolable if he loses him.'

George did not improve much during the day but he did not get any worse either. Teatime came and Mike's dad came to pick him up again Mike refused to leave George he wanted to stay with him through the night.

'Mike you have to come home I cannot leave you here all night your mother will be worried sick.'

'I want to stay with George.'

Mike argued and argued but his dad refused to let him stay, Al said she would come back later and check on George and would call Mike if there were any problems, Mike eventually agreed to go home. George had stopped groaning and was more settled however he still had not got up by the time Al had left.

'What's up with George Daff?'
'I don't know he has a belly ache but I think it is more than that, I did tell him not to pig out on that pile of grass we found.'
'George, George?' Whickered Lyric
'Do think he is still with us?'

Later that night torch light shone across the yard, George's stable door was opened and a small figure crept inside, it was Mike.

'Hi Georgie, how are you my little man?'

George blinked as the light shone in his eyes he was standing up so Mike moved the bale of straw to one side; the bran mash still had not been eaten. Mike got his sleeping bag which he had brought with him and laid it in George's stable, George laid down again and they both fell asleep, side by side.

Later that morning Trace and Al arrived on the yard to turn the horses out.

'Trace we have a visitor, I knew he would be here, he must be frozen as well as hungry.'

'I don't think so he obviously brought a supply of food as well as a flask.'

'Mike, Mike, wake up.'

'What, is something wrong with George?'

'No, he seems a lot better but you should not have come here during the night, you never know who is around and I bet you didn't leave a note for your parents, I will give them a call now.'

'I did leave a note, I could not sleep, and I wanted to be with George, is he really better?'

'He's not out of the woods yet but at least he is standing up and eating the bran mash, I will call your parents anyway.'

'Do you want a cup of tea Mike?'

'Yes please.'

Al and Trace turned out the other horses leaving George in. Al telephoned the vet who said George could be walked out if he wanted to and given a small amount of hay, Mike put George's head-collar on and walked him round the yard. Gradually over the next few days George was given more hay and then feed. Once George was back to his old self, Mike turned him out with the other horses.

'Nice to have you back George?' Lyric whickered.

'It's good to be back, I thought they were going to keep me in forever'

'So what has been going on while I have been away?' asked George as he chomped on some grass.

'Not a lot, it's just been the usual turn out, eat, play, eat some more, then go in. Bit boring really.' Dafydd snorted.

'Well why don't we find a few loose posts and see if we can break some rails and give the mistresses something to do?' George chortled.

'Good idea George, now I know why we have been bored, Georgie was missing.' Lennie smirked.

CHAPTER FIVE

HORSES ARE NOT ALWAYS FUN

'Hi Lucy, are you riding today?'

'Yes I thought I would ride round the fields.'

'Do you want me to come with you?'

'No, I want to do it on my own; I'm not a baby you know.'

Lucy had only been riding a little while and was not very confident. The older girls had taken it in turns to teach her how to ride, or in other words how to stay on while moving forward on a horse, as she could not afford proper lessons. Lucy now felt confident enough to ride Midge around the fields on her own instead of being on a lead rope.

Lucy went to get Midge in; Midge however preferred to remain out with her friends and so would not be caught. Every time Lucy got near, Midge would trot off until she was far enough away and then stop, when Lucy caught up Midge would run off again, Lucy gave up and returned to the yard.

'Alison would you catch Midge for me she keeps running off?'

'All right Lucy, let me get some feed to catch her with.'

Al did not like rewarding bad behaviour but it was the only way to catch Midge as her love of food exceeded her stubbornness to be caught. After a few attempts at running away Midge could no longer ignore the bucket of food, as soon as she stuck her head in the bucket Al secured the head-collar much to Midge's disgust.

Lucy groomed Midge, picked her hooves out and then put on the saddle and bridle, Lucy put on her hat and riding boots and got on Midge. She went in the sand school first and then she went into the fields.

'Hi Al, are you riding out today?'

'Hi Jill, no I'm going to use the sand school when Lucy has finished riding.'

'Is Lucy riding on her own?'

'Yes, she wanted to, she is in the sand school at the moment, so she should be all right.'

'How is Dancer going?'

'The same as usual, I don't suppose you could lend me your draw-rein later and show me how to use it?'

'Yes Jill, no problem.'

Jill got her head-collar and went to catch Dancer. Al finished sweeping the yard which was one of her pet hates, as soon as she had swept it you could guarantee that someone would either drop hay all over it, because they were too lazy to use a wheelbarrow or pick their horses hooves out without clearing it up. The other thing that annoyed Al was the soaking of hay; the yard was always waterlogged because people could not keep the drain clear of hay so it overflowed.

'Al quick, Lucy is on the ground, Midge has thrown her off.'

Al ran towards Jill and they both went to Lucy who was on the ground crying, Midge was over the other side of the field grazing away quite happily.

'Lucy are you all right?'

'I just wanted to canter and Midge threw me off.' Lucy sniffed and tried to get up.

'No don't move, are you bleeding anywhere or is there anything you cannot move?'

'My ankle hurts, I tried to stay on but Midge kept on bucking and I fell off.'

'I'm going to take your boot off.'

Al slowly removed Lucy's boot and sock; Lucy's ankle was red and starting to swell.

'Right, can you stand up Lucy, lean on me.'

Lucy stood up but could not put her foot on the ground.

'Jill give me a hand and help me get Lucy to my van and I will take her to hospital so her ankle can be x-rayed.'

Al put Lucy in her van and drove her to hospital and then waited while Lucy was checked out. Lucy was eventually x-rayed which showed that Lucy's ankle was not broken; it seemed that she had torn some muscles and ligaments. Al took Lucy home and explained to her mum what had happened she then returned to the yard to find that Jill had untacked Midge and had ridden Dancer.

'Perhaps we could try the draw-rein tomorrow Al. How is Lucy?'

'She is fine, her ankle was not broken just badly sprained, better safe then sorry.'

'I bet her parents won't be allowing her near horses again!'

'I don't think they will have a lot of choice you know how difficult kids can be when they want something.'

The horses were brought in, fed and rugged.

> 'Midge you are horrible, that was really mean throwing Lucy off, she was just getting her confidence.' Lyric whinnied.
>
> 'I say start as you mean to go on, it's better that I throw her off now instead of later. Anyway I should have been retired years ago.'
>
> 'Well when you're left out in the cold, your feet aren't trimmed and your not fed you will soon wish you had not thrown her off.' George knew this from experience.

As Lucy was unable to attend to Midge so it fell to Al and Trace to muck her out and feed her.

'Al have we got room for another horse?'

'Why do you ask Trace?'

'I have a friend called Gayle, I know her from a previous yard. She doesn't like where she is, the yard owner wont let them help each other out and charges them for everything, so she wants to move.'

'What she got?'

'She has a three year old Part Bred Arab called Tucker she's breaking in, she's really nice.'

'All right she can come on a month's trial; I bet Sarah won't be pleased.'

Three days later Gayle arrived with Tucker in her own horsebox. As with all new arrivals he was put in a stable and wormed. Tucker was 15 hands and a chestnut with a blaze he was put in the stable between Primrose and Dancer.

'Hi I'm Alison, call me Al.'

'Hi I'm Gayle and this is Tucker.'

'Is that your own box?'

'Yes, my dad bought it for me, it needed some work done to it but it carries two horses with no problem at all.'

'A word of warning, should you decide to go to a show there are some others here who do not have transport and will be wanting to join you.'

'Oh I know, I had that at my other place, it's not a problem, I like the company and it helps with the running costs.'

'We all bed down on straw here, if you don't have any I can sell you a few bales until you can get some or I can order some for you.'

'The thing is Tucker is called Tucker for a reason, he eats anything including his bed so I have to bed down on shavings, is that a problem?'

'I don't think so, I'm just about to make a cup of tea would you like one?'

'Yes please it's been quite a day.'

Al made the tea while Gayle settled Tucker in his box and wormed him. Al showed Gayle around the yard.

'You can put your saddle in here, it is secure. This is the canteen, we have a tea fund of fifty pence each per week, your feed goes in here and so do rugs.'

'Do I get my own feed or is it bulk ordered?'

'Either, I can order for you just let me know what you want. All areas must be kept clean. Hay and Straw goes next door in the barn, you will have your own-sectioned area.'

'What is the vermin population like around here?'

'Do you mean human or rodent . . . no only kidding; we don't have many the local cat population keeps them down. The jumps are in this arena and next to it the schooling arena, this one is floodlit.'

'What fields are being used at the moment?'

'We have just moved the horses to the middle field for the next few months. I would like to divide up the big field but I don't have the time or the timber.'

As the girls were talking a fight broke out in the field between Dancer and Dafydd by the time the girls got to the fence the dust had settled but Dancer was limping. Al went and got Dancer's head-collar, at first he did not want to be caught but he could not run off so gave up and allowed the head-collar to be put on. Al took him back to the yard and hosed the mud off his front leg; once the leg was clean Al could see a lump and a cut that was bleeding.

'Gayle can you get the medical kit, it's in the feed room by the sink?'

'Ok, shouldn't you call his owner?'

'I will once I have sorted him out, she wouldn't know what to do anyway!'

Al made sure there wasn't anything in the wound and then put on some antiseptic powder, lint and a bandage she then put him in the sand school so that he would not become stiff and get into further trouble with the other horses. Al cleared away the medial kit and then went to check on the other horses, the only injury was a loss of hair on Daff's face!

'Pulled one too many faces did he Daff, stay out of trouble you or I will have to put you on your own!'

Daff nudged Al and then laid his muzzle on her shoulder his big brown eyes looked at Al; Daff seemed to know that this tactic would always get him out of trouble. Al got out her mobile and called Jill to let her know what had happened to Dancer, as predicted Jill said she would be right down even though there was no reason for her to leave work as there was nothing she could do. Daff realising he was not in trouble then proceeded to shove his nose into Al's pocket for a mint or anything that was edible.

'You've got a cheek; you beat up Dancer then expect a reward. Mind you I think if was a horse Dancer would be the one I would beat up too, have a mint.'

Jill arrived and started to pamper Dancer who took full advantage of his mistress and put the limp on even more.

'I think I should call the vet, he should be in resting . . . my poor baby.'

'Jill he's been kicked nothing is broken, he's just bruised with a small cut which I have treated. If you put him in he will seize up, its better that he walks round.'

'Who kicked him?'

'I don't know and it doesn't matter, horses will be horses!'

As evening came the other owners arrived to exercise their horses and put them to bed. Al brought Daff in, who as he passed Dancer, put his ears back and lunged at him.

'Well I think we know who was responsible for Dancer's bad leg.' Jill glared.

'Jill my horse has a lump of hair missing from his face, it is more then likely that Dancer bit him and then Daff kicked Dancer who in the end came off worse.'

The horses gradually settled down for the night.

'That sorted you out Dancer, next time it will be more then one leg if you try and bite me again.' Daff snorted.

'I found that piece of bread you had no right to take it.' Dancer retorted.

'I have been here the longest and I am older then you, where's your respect?'

'Respect is earned, you are nothing but an overweight donkey, I can outrun you and out jump you so you must respect me!'

'Who's the one with the worst injury?'

'Oi you two, you are as bad as each other, if you are not careful one of you will have to leave if you keep injuring one another.' Lyric advised.

'Enough of that you two, who are you?' George had spotted a new face.

'I'm Tucker I arrived today.'

'Hi I'm George, take no notice of these two they are always arguing. What's your favourite sport?'

'I don't know, my mistress has only just started getting on me. I don't like the thing she puts in my mouth though!'

'Don't worry you will get use to that, is yours metal or rubber?'

'It's soft and black' Tucker said through a mouthful of hay.

'That's rubber, they are the best, and it doesn't take so long to chew through them!' Daff whinnied.

CHAPTER SIX

FENCE REPAIRS ARE NEVER ENDING

'Not again, I'm fed up with repairing the fences around here!'

Whenever a fence post was broken or a rail had been snapped it was always left to Al and Trace to repair them, everyone else would be too busy or they could not possibly hit a nail with a hammer because they did not know how to!

'Trace give me a hand to replace a post and I think we are going to need two rails.'

'We have only got one rail and the post we have is a bit rotten.'

'That would not surprise me, I think it's time we rummaged through the local skips for any discarded timber. We will have to brace one of the rails, we do have some nails don't we?'

'Well we have some two inch nails but no three or four inch, I guess we are going to have straighten the ones we take out!'

Al and Trace put the tools and timber in a wheelbarrow along with a flask of tea and some biscuits as lunch was approaching and the fence to be repaired was at the back of middle field, well it wouldn't be at the front that would be too easy! The broken post had to be removed for the new post to be put in; this was the worst job. Once the broken post is removed the new one can be put in and the rails nailed on.

'Whoever pulls the short straw gets to dig the post out!'

'I knew it would be me.' Trace groaned.

'While you do that I will try and repair the rail and straighten the nails.'

The horses watched as the girls repaired the fence; it was as though they were waiting for the girls to finish so they could inspect the work and try to break it again. Daff was particularly good at this, he would walk along and lean on each rail until one wobbled, this indicated that the post was loose or on the verge of breaking. He would then lean on it until it gave way, sometimes only one rail would break this meant that Daff would have to jump over the bottom rail, which wasn't a problem for him.

'There that should hold for a while.'

'You think so, Daff is already wondering how he is going to break it.'

'He's a little devil, to think of the problems I have had in getting him to jump and yet he doesn't think twice about breaking rails and jumping them!'

'Now Lennie's here I think we are going to have our work cut out.'

'Robert can get his finger out and do some repairs, you never know we might be able to get his brother to help . . . we can repair in a foursome then.'

'Behave yourself Al; we would never get the fence fixed if both of them were here!'

'Do we dare check the rest of the posts, or is that just looking for extra work?'

As the girls walked back they pushed each post to see if it wobbled, a few posts were a little lose but none were broken, yet! Once the girls were out of sight the horses started to inspect the repaired fencing.

'Daff do you think you could make a better job of it next time!' Lyric asked sarcastically.

'I did my best, some of the other posts are lose I will try one of them next.'

'Lennie come and lean on this post.' Lyric whinnied.

Lennie leaned differently to Daff; he placed his behind on the post whereas Daff used his chest. Slowly the post started to crack until it eventually broke. One by one the horses wandered into the field.

'Al, you won't believe this they have done it again!'

'You are joking, well we can't do any more repairs we do not have any timber. We are going to have to get some barbed wire; they have no respect for rails.'

'I agree, it's either that or electric fencing and we certainly do not have any money in the kitty for electric fencing.'

'We will have to start selling more manure, let's bag some up and put it by the road.'

The girls bagged up the manure in old feed bags and put a sign up selling it for a pound a bag. The local residents knew that the girls had to do repairs and pay for the materials so they would often buy manure for fifty pence per barrow load, one resident used his wheelie-bin; after the rubbish men had emptied it, to transport the manure to his garden!

'Hey Al, there is a skip just down the road they are renovating a house that might have some wood in it.'

'Let's go and have a look is it in walking distance?'

'Yes, we can have a look and if there is anything of use we can come back and get the car.'

Al and Trace noticed timber poking out of the skip.

'Oi, what do you think you're up to?' A voice barked from the house.

'We were wondering if you wanted this timber, only our horses have broken the fence and we do not have anything to repair it with.' Trace was putting on the hard done by look.

'We can't offer money but we do have some manure!' Al added her bit, trying to win a sympathy vote.

'It's all right; help yourselves, the more you take the more space I will have to put rubbish in.'

Al pulled the timber from the skip while Trace went back and got her Land Rover, the timbers had nails in, which would annoy some people but to Al it was an added bonus as they now had nails as well as timber.

'Hey Al there is a sink in here, we could replace the one in the feed room and look here is a cupboard.'

'Excuse me; can we have some other bits as well?' Al pleaded.

'Take what you want.' The builder replied.

Al and Trace were in heaven they piled anything that thought would be useful into the car, they put in so much that Al had to walk back to the yard. Once back at the yard they unloaded and pulled the nails from the timber.

'Hi girls what have you been up to?' Robert asked.

'Just in time, here Robert as I pull the nails out you can straighten them and put them in the correct tins.'

Robert knew better then to make excuses or refuse so he used a hammer and straightened the nails on a brick and then put them in the correct tin according to the length of the nail. The timber was then measured and the length was written in chalk on each piece of wood, it was then stacked in the tool shed.

'It's too late today to repair that fence; we will have to do it tomorrow. Robert when are you free, before you answer that, it was your horse that broke through the fence!'

'I guess I could be down here tomorrow lunchtime.'

'Are you riding Trace?'

'No I'm too tired I might lunge.'

Trace went to get Lyric in and Al finished laying her bed, Daff came in with a very contented look on his face, as did all the horses.

'Did you notice Daff that they did not repair the fence we broke this afternoon?'

'Yes, means we will get another day at least in that field.'

'I noticed George scratching himself on a post the other side of the field and it was wobbling.'

'Show it to me tomorrow. Hey Tucker you're a bit quiet, what's up?'

'I think I ate something that disagreed with me.'

'Teach you a lesson for being so greedy.' Prim sneered.

Next day Sarah turned out the horses, who immediately headed for the broken fence, even though the field they were breaking into had less grass then the field they were in. Sarah pretended she did not notice and left before Al or Trace arrived otherwise she would end up helping with repairs and that just would not do as Sarah had just painted her nails! Later that day Al and Trace arrived and gathered the tools and timber together.

'Look what I bought Trace.'

'Who paid for that, there isn't any money?'

'I paid for it myself, in the long run it's got to be cheaper then having to keep on replacing rails.'

Al had bought a reel of barbed wire and staples to run along the top of the fence. The girls made a flask of tea and some sandwiches and put everything in the wheelbarrow.

'Hey Trace why don't we do this in style and put everything in your Land Rover it would be a lot easier then the wheelbarrow?'

'All right on the condition you help me clean it out when we have finished.'

'Agreed.'

Al and Trace put everything into the Land Rover and drove up the field. They drew straws and this time Al got the job of digging the post out. Once the post was out and the new one was in they nailed the rails on.

'I though Robert was supposed to be here to give us a hand.'

'You must be joking Trace, he's a bloke you didn't really think he would turn up, not if it meant he had to do some work!'

'But it was his horse that broke it.'

'Yes and his horse will probably break the next one as well, if Daff doesn't do it first.'

'Right, now the rails are up we can put the barbed wire on. Trace, take the reel down there after I have stapled it on at this end and pull it as tight as you can.'

Trace pulled on the barbed wire to make it as taught as she could and Al stapled it onto the top rail. The horses were watching this; they had seen barbed wire before and knew that their days were numbered for breaking that fence in the future. When Trace and Al had run out of barbed wire they packed everything up and drove back to the yard.

'That should stop them for a while. Oh look who has turned up, good evening Robert.' Al said sarcastically.

'Evening, but it's only three in the afternoon!' Robert replied.

'Yes, well past lunchtime, so where were you?'

'My mum insisted that I had to do some jobs before I could go out, but I'm here now.'

'But we have done the fencing, so you can muck out our horses instead, while we ride.'

Al and Trace tacked up Daff and Lyric and went for a ride over the common while Robert mucked out.

'Robert, why are you mucking Daff out?' Sarah enquired.

'I was supposed to help with the fence repair but I turned up too late so I get to muck out instead.'

'I don't know why you allow them to bully you, I wouldn't stand for it.'

'Because I like them and it was my horse who broke the fence so I should have helped.'

'Well if you want to be a mouse instead of a man that is up to you.'

As Sarah walked away Robert made a few gestures of his own, which he would never do in front of Sarah. Robert also soaked Daff and Lyric's hay and changed their water ready for them when they got back, then he attended to his own stable. Sarah mucked out and then got Prim in to lunge, unfortunately she forgot to shut her stable door and when she returned Midge had helped herself to Prim's hay and she had mucked up her bed. Sarah's bed was laid perfectly flat, the walls were laid as though they had been measured and then checked with a spirit level, Sarah chased Midge out and then laid her bed again. Mike arrived with a big bag of fish and chips, the smell wafted across the yard.

'Hello Mike my old chum, give us a chip.' Robert grovelled.

'Creep, go on then just one.'

Robert grabbed a couple of chips with his mucky hands.

'Oh you are disgusting Robert, you have been mucking out and then you eat with your hands before you have washed them.' Sarah recoiled in horror.

'Why do want a chip as well, here have one of mine.' Robert offered.

'Don't be so horrible Robert you know how stuck up girls are.' Mike chuckled.

Al and Trace returned to the yard and were amazed to find that their stables were all ready, Al's nose picked up the smell of chips.

'Right who's got chips on the yard?'

'I have.' Mike replied.

'Give them here, chips aren't allowed, yard rule.'

'Mike handed over his dinner.'

'Al don't be so rotten leave the lad alone.' Trace said.

'Only joking you idiot, here I don't want them, well not all of them.' Al grabbed a chip.

'Oh how could you eat those chips after Robert put his mucky hands in them?' Sarah grimaced.

'Nothing wrong with a bit of muck, you are too picky Sarah.'

'Right I'm dying for a cup of tea, who is making it?'

'I will.' Mike volunteered.

'Robert did you do all this?'

'Yes, I didn't feel like riding so I thought I would do your entire stable, since you helped me with Lennie and repaired the fencing.'

'Oh you little sweetie, here let me give you a big wet thank you kiss.' Al lunged towards Robert, who ran as fast as he could.

'That's all right, you have thanked me enough.' Robert yelled.

Mike made the tea and everyone went to the feed room for their drink. The fencing was discussed, Sarah objected to the barbed wire in case Prim hurt herself, Al explained that broken posts and rails were more hazardous and it was the only way to prevent the horses form destroying all the fencing. Once the tea was drunk everyone finished their horses off and went home.

'Well, we will have to start on the other fence now they have used that prickly wire.' Daff snorted.
'I noticed that your mistress Prim ignored the broken fence this morning, she is a right lazy . . . .'
'Shut up you, my mistress didn't have time to repair the fence she's far too busy, besides I didn't break it!' Prim snorted.
'No, but you went through with the rest of us.' Dancer chipped in.
'Lennie, did you deliberately tread on her foot when she turned you out this morning or was it an accident?'
'It was an accident; mistresses' feet are so tiny you just don't notice them until it's too late!'

CHAPTER SEVEN

TANTRUMS

'You are not the boss here you know, so don't try and tell me what to do.' Sarah snapped.

'I only asked if you were able to use a broom and if so could you sweep up the hay that you have left on the floor along with Prims droppings.' Robert retorted.

'I will clean it up when I am ready not when you tell me.'

'But it has been here since this morning.'

'Hey, what's all the shouting about?' Al enquired.

'This little chauvinist is trying to tell me what to do.'

'Robert what have you been saying to upset Sarah?'

'Nothing, her horse messed on the yard this morning and then she dropped her hay and she has just left it for someone else to clear up.'

'I was about to clean it up when you opened your mouth.'

'Rubbish you were about to leave, your horse is all done and you have put your tools away.'

'Right, that is enough. This yard works on co-operation, you must clear up your own mess and your horses when it happens not several hours later, so go and get your tools Sarah and clear this mess up and don't leave it for someone else. Robert if you have a problem come and see me about it, do not start a shouting match on the yard.'

Sweeping the yard was always a sore point as everyone liked a clean yard but no-one was prepared to keep it clean as usual it was always left to the dedicated few. Sarah swept up the mess and then quickly put it in Gayle's wheelbarrow as she was still mucking out.

'You lazy, stuck up.'

'Robert what is going on now?' Al intervened.

'She has just put her muck in Gayle's wheelbarrow.'

'Gayle doesn't mind, do you Gayle?' Sarah glared at Gayle.

'Well no, as long as I can get all my muck in without making two trips.'

'See, so what is the problem Robert?' Sarah smiled.

'Robert go and attend to your own horse and ignore Sarah, she is just trying to wind you up and you are falling for it.'

Robert left mumbling to himself that he was going to teach Sarah a lesson sooner rather then later. Al returned to Daff as she was about to ride in the sand school. Al enjoyed flat work, the others preferred jumping or going for a hack as flat work was boring, Al's reply to this was that if it was boring then they weren't doing it properly. Daff was capable of many disciplines but he excelled at Dressage this was mainly due to Alison's determination and her instructor, who was amazed at how Daff and Al had progressed over the years.

'I take it you are not in a very good mood today Daff, It's no good shaking your head you are going to give me collection if we are here all day.'

**'Oh you think so do you, push me too far and
I will throw you off.'**

'Oh no you don't, your backside is staying where it belongs near to the ground and not in the air.'

Daff stuck his head between his legs, as he just was not in the mood to be co-operative, Al pushed him on as a horse is supposed to find it very difficult to buck while moving forward, it is a shame someone did not tell Daff this! Daff exploded bucking and twisting just like a two-year-old child throwing a fit on the floor. He then leapt forward but was restrained by the draw-rein, after a few minutes he stopped and began to respond to Al's requests.

**'There that showed you what
I can do, so don't push me again!'**

'Right now you have got that out of your system can we do some work?'

Daff always worked much better when he had finished his tantrum this was either because he had worn himself out or realised he was not going to win. Al did some shoulder-in, leg yielding and half-pass, once they had warmed up 20 metre circles and three loop serpentines then some acute transitions walk to canter and halts as well as some rein back and the most forgotten of all gaits the free walk. So many riders lost marks in Dressage tests because of their poor free walk quite often the horses would not walkout as they were so use to hanging on the bit.

One of things that really irritated Al were poles and other equipment being left out in the arena, a notice had been put up stating that all equipment must be put away after use but it would appear that not many people could read!

'Hi Al, how is he going?'

'Hi Trace, very well after a little tantrum, are you riding?'

'Yes, I will probably school after you have finished. What is up with Robert?'

'Sarah has been winding him up by leaving a mess on the yard.'

'Not again, she can be a complete cow, do you not think that we should ask her to leave.'

'We could do let see what happens, she was here before Robert so in fairness we should ask him to leave. Do you know who left the trotting poles out?'

'I think Sarah was in here last, see what I mean she seems to upset someone practically every day. Do you want a cup of tea?'

'No thanks, I want to ride for another ten minutes or until he is fully co-operative.'

Gayle had finished mucking out and was grooming Tucker ready to lunge him in his tack so she could ride for a little while afterwards.

'Hi Gayle, how is his training going?'

'Hi Trace, well he hasn't done much so far but he has been very good with the saddle and the bit, so I am just going to lunge him and then get on him.'

'Have you sat on him before?'

'Only briefly, I just laid my weight across him. Would you help me when I get on him by holding on to the lunge?'

'Yes sure, Al is in the arena at the moment she will be another ten minutes or so.'

Gayle took Tucker to the sand school after Al had finished and began to lunge him. Tucker began well then started to canter and would not stop. Gayle decided not to stop him but to let him go for as long as he wanted to, this was mainly so that he would tire himself out and be less resistant to Gayle getting on. Once he had done ten minutes on either rein Gayle decided to get on.

'Trace are you free.' Gayle shouted.

'Yes dear I'm free, go on get your backside up there, here I will give you a leg up. Just lay across him first then slowly sit up.'

'Just you keep hold of that rein in case he starts.'

Gayle gradually sat up in the saddle, Tuckers ears went back and he looked round wondering why his mistress was on him. Trace walked him forward, Tucker was a little unbalanced at first but soon became accustomed to the weight on his back.

'Gayle take the reins in your hands and slowly take a contact.'

'All right, don't you let go of that rein.'

'I won't, just relax he is taking to this very well. As I give a command verbally you must use your legs and seat and give the correct physical command so he understands what they mean.'

'Only walking, no trotting.' Gayle insisted nervously.

As Trace gave the voice command to walk on Gayle used her legs, after ten minutes or so Gayle got off making sure her legs did not hit Tucker's back as she swung her leg over.

'There that wasn't so bad was it?'

'No, but it felt really strange getting on him, I have only led and groomed him for the past three years and to be above him was weird.'

'It is going to take time and patience but the rewards are worth it. If you did this everyday it won't be long before you are cantering him.'

'Thanks Trace, would you help me tomorrow?'

'Al is doing Lyric for me tomorrow as I have to go to London, ask her to help you, she trained Daff herself so she will know what to do.'

Gayle took Tucker back to his stable and gave him his tea.

'Hey Tucker, how did you like your mistress getting on you?' Daff whinnied.

'She was very heavy, and it felt really strange her being above and behind me and then she pulled on the thing in my mouth and that wasn't very nice!'

'You will get use to that, what you want to do is to give her the idea you are co-operating and then when she least expects it, you know relaxed, throw her off with a bit of luck she may be too scared to get back on!'

'Daff that's not a very good example to set, Tucker is only young. Take no notice of him, be nice to your mistress and you will get to go places and have fun with her.' Lyric corrected.

'Lyric's right, I was only pulling your leg. However you shouldn't be too nice otherwise she will take advantage.'

'What will she do next?'

'She will do the same again as she did today and then you will trot and then canter depending how you cope with it and whether she has the courage to ask!'

The following evening Gayle got Tucker ready and after she had lunged Al helped her get on while she held the lunge. Tucker was more relaxed about having Gayle above him and so was more balanced as he walked round. Gayle had a very light contact as Tucker's mouth was still very soft and not use to someone pulling on the bit. Al asked Tucker to trot, as she did Gayle gave the leg command, Tucker trotted, Gayle did rising trot to allow Tucker to balance himself.

'That will do for today Gayle, he has gone very well.'

'Can't we try to canter him?'

'Not yet he is not settled in the trot yet, do this for the next few days and then we will try. The longer you take to get things the better and less resistant he will be. You have waited this long to get on don't ruin him now.'

For the rest of the week Gayle only walked and trotted Tucker off the lunge rein. Tucker was becoming use to his mistress on him; he did circles and loops with no problem at all. Gayle could not resist the urge to canter him and so sat in the trot and then asked for the canter. Tucker just ran faster as he did not understand what the leg command meant, Gayle asked again for a canter, Tucker was now getting upset because he did not understand so he stopped and reared, Gayle sat the rear and several more, eventually Tucker stopped.

'Now do you understand why I said you should wait?' Al said, she had been watching from afar.

'I couldn't resist I just wanted to see if he could canter.'

'You should have waited, I will get the lunge line and we will do this properly, now you have asked him you will have to get the canter.'

Al got the lunge line and attached it to Tucker's bridle.'

'Right, walk him on and then go to trot, when you hear my canter command you must give the physical command, if he does not canter I will crack the whip and you must be ready, as he may leap to the canter, just stay with him.'

Once Tucker had settled in the trot Al asked him to canter, Gayle asked with her legs but Tucker just went faster so Al asked again and cracked the whip. Tucker leapt to canter as Gayle continued to give the canter command after a few circles Tucker was asked to walk and the same was done on the other rein.

'Thanks Al, that was amazing.'

'The canter is the hardest thing for a young horse to do carrying a rider that is why I said to do walk and trot so he could get his balance and build his muscles with you on board. Continue with walk and trot and just a little canter and only on the lunge, as he still does not understand your command for canter.'

Gayle did as Al advised, either Al or Trace would hold the lunge while Tucker learnt the commands, eventually Tucker could be ridden without the lunge. The next stage was for Tucker to go out in company so Trace and Al tacked up their horses and rode out with Tucker and Gayle. They rode in single file with Tucker in the middle; Gayle had previously walked Tucker in hand along the roads. Tucker was a little wound up but was enjoying being ridden out. The girls rode along the road only walking and trotting, after half an hour they returned to the yard.

'I'm going to get you for that Robert, you wait and see.' Sarah screamed.

'Robert what have you done now?' Al sighed.

'He has been putting his horses' droppings in my stable instead of the muck heap, I wondered why Prim was making so much mess, and I thought there was something wrong with her.'

'Well she left her mess all over the yard, so I thought I would teach her a lesson.' Robert grinned.

'Right, either you two stop behaving like a couple of kids or one of you will have to leave.'

Robert and Sarah fell silent and returned to their stables, Trace, Al and Gayle untacked their horses and turned them out.

'That was a neat trick of Roberts to put Lennie's droppings in Prim's stable, I don't know how Sarah didn't notice as his droppings are twice the size of Prim's.' Al chuckled.

'I know, I could hardly keep a straight face. I wonder what the next trick will be.'

'I just hope things don't get out of hand, Robert sees it as a joke but Sarah doesn't see the funny side at all.'

'Tucker was very good wasn't he?'

'Yes but youngsters always seem to have a knack of catching you out when you least expect it.'

Trace and Al mucked out; Gayle had already done hers and was making cups of tea for everyone. Suddenly Dancer appeared snorting at the gate he had his saddle and bridle on but Jill was nowhere to be seen, he had blood dripping down his front leg.

'Does anyone know where Jill is or where she went?'

'I think she went to ride in the fields.' Robert replied.

'Right, everyone down tools and start checking the fields, Gayle and Sarah you check middle field, Robert you check the small and front fields, Trace and I will do big field. If you find her blow on your whistle, make sure you check in and around bushes and trees.'

Trace put Dancer in his stable and Al issued whistles, each pair split up and checked the perimeter of their field. After half an hour a whistle was heard from middle field, the other raced over to Gayle and Sarah who were trying to pull something from the bushes.

'Did you find her?'

'No we found her hat though and there are some fresh hoof marks here.'

'Right everyone lets check the woods, she may be concussed and wandering.'

Slowly the mistresses and master walked into the wood calling and searching for any signs of Jill, suddenly a whistle was heard.

'Robert that was right in my ear.' Sarah yelled.

'Robert there is no need to use your whistle when we are all so close.' Al advised.

'Sorry, I think Jill is over there.'

Robert had seen what appeared to be a pile of clothing, as they all approached Jill turned round; she was sitting on the ground crying.

'I'm lost.' Jill said as she burst into tears.

'It's all right Jill, come with us we will take you home.' Trace assisted Jill to stand up.

'Who are you, I don't know you, my mum said I'm not allowed to talk to strangers.'

'You have had an accident come with us back to the yard, Dancer is all right.'

'Dancer, I know Dancer.' Jill tried to remember.

Jill was helped back to the yard, her arm was bleeding and so Al took some baler twine from her pocket and made a sling to keep the arm up she also used some as a tourniquet to stop the bleeding. Trace dialled 999 and requested an ambulance to be sent to the yard. Jill kept on asking questions all the time but the questions made no sense, eventually they reached the yard. Jill was sat down and a blanket was put round her to keep her warm, Al released the tourniquet and bandaged Jill's arm. The ambulance arrived and backed up to the yard gate.

'Hi what have we got here then?' The paramedic enquired.

'This is Jill, we are not certain as to what happened, her horse came back to the yard without her. We think he threw her and she must have hit a tree as we found her hat then her, she doesn't make any sense and she has a nasty gash to her arm.'

The ambulance crew checked Jill over and put on a neck brace as a precaution and then they put her in the ambulance and took her to hospital.

'Well done everyone, I suppose we will never know what happened.'

'Wasn't Jill strange, stranger then normal I mean!'

'That's the result of a concussion, she probably won't remember anything that has happened, let's check on Dancer.'

Trace got Dancer out and hosed his leg off while Al got the medical kit.

'It's nasty Al; I wonder how he did it?'

'At least it's a clean cut and fortunately on the front of the leg, let's just clean and bandage it as Jill is short of cash at the moment and can't afford a vet's bill, what do you think?'

'We will probably get away with bandaging; if it doesn't heal then a vet will have to be called, At least he has a matching pair of scars now!'

Trace and Al cleaned the wound and applied an antiseptic powder, they then bandaged it and did the same on his other leg so his circulation was not affected and put Dancer in his stable.

Once all the horses had been attended to Al and Trace went to the hospital to check on Jill. The doctor told them that Jill would be released when she made sense, Al quipped that would be never as Jill never made sense! The cut on her arm had been stitched and there were no broken bones just bruises and minor cuts and a concussion.

Trace and Al went to see Jill but she was asleep.

Back at the yard the horses were reflecting on the days events.

'Right Dancer what have you been up to?' Lyric quizzed.

'I'm not sure I was cantering along and something hit my leg which tripped me up, my mistress went flying and hit a tree. I got up and ran back to the yard.'

'Yeah more like you had a tantrum and threw her off!'

'No honest, I got the shock of my life when I hit the ground nose first, my leg really hurts.'

'Its not good news when that blue light van turns up, I knew a horse whose rider came off and was put in that van, she was never seen again, the horse disappeared as well.'

'Don't say that.' Dancer whinnied.

'Well that will teach you a lesson for throwing your rider.' Daff smirked.

'But it wasn't my fault!'

'I bet you don't see her again Dancer, then you will be going.'

Jill was kept in hospital for four days, which worried Dancer as he thought that he would never see her again. Jill did not remember what had happened but a visit to the field by Al and Trace found a loop of wire imbedded in the ground, which must have caught Dancer's leg and resulted in Jill being thrown off!

CHAPTER EIGHT

WHO DARES WINS

'Hey Al, have you seen this team competition for yards, each yard sends a team of three riders and horses to compete in three events, show-jumping, dressage and showing?' Trace asked.

'Yes I saw a poster at the tack shop; we don't have any riders and horses that can compete at that level!'

'Well I could do the show-jumping, Sarah could do the showing and you could do the dressage, come on it would be a laugh, besides there is £300.00 prize money which we could use to buy materials for the yard.' Trace pleaded.

'Um, I suppose we could give it a go we have nothing to lose except the entry fees, when is it?'

'It's in two weeks time, entries close this Wednesday.'

'Well that's pushing it; we will never be ready in time!'

'So, we are unlikely to win anyway, let's just go and have some fun!'

The girls grabbed Sarah as she arrived; Sarah would never miss a chance to show off and agreed to complete the team. They filled in the entry forms, Al was doing Novice Test 24 and Trace was jumping the 2'6 course, Sarah had entered the Arab in hand. They started to prepare for the event which took place over two days; this meant that they had to take food and sleeping bags for themselves as well as all the equipment for the horses.

'What's all the fuss about?' Robert enquired.

'We are preparing for a two day team event.' Sarah replied.

'Can Lennie and I compete too?'

'No, it's for Alison, Tracy and myself as we are at a level which is superior to yours, that nag of yours would be totally out of place at a two day event!' Sarah stuck her nose in the air and walked away before Robert could reply.

'Take no notice Robert, we have to have horses that are able to jump, show and do dressage, if cart pulling was a class Lennie would be going. Would you like to come with us and be our groom?' Al asked.

'All right but Sarah can find another groom, I'm not fetching and carrying for that ungrateful stuck up.'

'Now, now Robert you are going to have to find away of dealing with Sarah's attitude, the more she gets to you the worse she will be.'

'I know but I can't help it she really winds me up.'

Over the next two weeks the girls practised until they knew what they were doing backwards, they prepared Sarah's lorry to take Prim and all the hay and feed they would need as well as buckets, blankets and tack. The sleeping bags and 'human' necessities would be put in Tracy's Land Rover and this would pull Daff and Lyric in the trailer. It was decided that they would all go to the event the day before so that they would not be rushing around on the day and the horses would be more settled.

Friday came and the girls loaded their horses and set off for the event. It would take about an hour and a half to get to the show ground, Trace took the lead with Al navigating and Robert in the back, Sarah followed behind. Once at the show-ground the girls were directed to an area where they could park and unload their horses. The organisers had erected electric fencing in squares so the competing horses could be 'turned out' as stables were in short supply and were only available to those who paid an additional fee. The girls put their horses in the grazing area, Daff went straight to the fencing to go through it and got a nasty shock, which was painful but not dangerous, the horses settled down and the girls unpacked their equipment

'Hey Sarah are you sleeping in your lorry or joining us in our tent?' Al enquired.

'I'm not sleeping on the ground with all the creepy-crawlies and bugs; I have a folding bed in my lorry so I will be sleeping in there!'

'I know she doesn't like Robert but he's not a creepy-crawly, anyway Al you know very well that Sarah has her own private quarters and would not be seen dead sleeping with us lowly persons!' Trace grinned.

'I know, I just like winding her up. Trace hold this pole while I secure the tent. What we having for tea then?'

'Well we are camping so I suppose it will be bangers and beans with a mug of tea.'

'Oh, Sarah will love that, I bet she has already made her tea, it's probably smoked salmon with petite poi's and french fries with a chilled white wine!'

'I like bangers and beans.' Robert chipped in.

'Bangers and beans it is then, Robert can you get the cooking stuff out and set it up well away from the tent and somewhere sheltered.'

'Yes sure.'

Robert got the gas stove and utensils out along with the food, he did think about setting it up in the back of Sarah's lorry but decided that was not a good idea and so laid everything out in the back of the trailer. He left enough room for his sleeping bag as Robert did not have a tent and did not want to squeeze in with Trace and Al as this would set tongues wagging especially Sarah's! While Robert started the cooking the girls made the horses their teas and hayed them, after a good brush the horses were rugged up and the girls went to get their dinner. Robert enjoyed cooking and was thinking of training to become a chef; he had cooked sausages, bacon, egg, hash browns and beans with a large pot of tea.

'Wow that looks really tasty Robert.'

'Thanks, here's yours Trace and yours Al, Sarah do you want some?'

'I, I.' Trace and Al glared at Sarah

'Thank you Robert I would love to sample your cooking.'

'Robert did you do any bread and butter?'

'Yes Al, it's behind me.'

'Oh no Daff heard the B word Al!'

Daff trotted up to the fence tossing his head, which was his way of demanding that he had some, Al threw a few slices of bread over the fence to satisfy Daff's demands.

'Pity we can't have a camp fire that would really make it feel like camping.'

'We would also need someone playing a harmonica or guitar for a sing song.' Trace added.

'Oh please, this is a two day equestrian event, not Woodstock you know!'

'Sarah you are such a stuck up prude, were you dropped on your head at some point in your life, what makes you think you are superior to us, after all your horse is kept on a D.I.Y yard!'

'I may not have the financial status but I do have the etiquette to drag myself out of the gutter!'

'It's a good job that I am able to rise above such comments otherwise you would be sucking your beans through a straw. You may think you have etiquette but you do not, you are rude and have no personal skills what so ever. I have tolerated your airs and graces but even I am now becoming tired of it, as are the other horse owners on the yard. If you do not stop the insults then you will have to stable your horse somewhere else.' With that Al got up to clean her plate.

'Well you have certainly done it now Sarah, you are way over the top.' Trace got up and left.

'See what you have done now, this was meant to be a team and you ruined it Sarah.' Robert growled.

'I speak as I find, I cannot help it if they are sensitive to criticism.'

'That's just it though, you insult you don't criticise, there is a difference.'

'I do not need a 'boy' to advise me as to what I should say and think!'

'Well somebody should before you end up all on your own with only Prim to talk to.'

Sarah glared at Robert and then put her plate down and retired to her lorry. Robert cleared away the pots while Al and Trace lit the Tilley lamps as it was getting dark. Tilley lamps run on paraffin and last for hours whereas torches run out, plus Tilley's give off a great deal of heat, which is appreciated on a chilly night.

'You all right Al.' Trace asked.

'Yeah, you don't think I would allow a stuck up madam like her to get to me do you?'

'No, but it is a shame that it happened now when we could have had such fun.'

'I know, but someone had to stop her, I just don't understand how she can be so nasty?'

'May be she will have a think and change.'

'Don't you bet on it, what's that noise?'

Robert had got out his guitar and was playing it, Trace and Al put the Tilley lamps on the ground together, which made it seem like there was a camp fire and sat around listening to Robert play.

'How long have you been playing the guitar Robert?'

'A few years, my brother taught me, he is really good.'

Al and Trace put in requests for different tunes, and sang to bits they knew. Eventually they retired to their sleeping bags as tomorrow would be a long day.

'Hey Daff do you reckon this is our new home?' Prim whinnied.

'No, I think we are here to do some work, I have been doing flat work all week.'

'And I have been jumping quite a bit.' Lyric added.

'How's your nose after hitting that fencing Daff?'
Lyric enquired.

'It's all right, I thought it was a thin piece of fencing
that would not be a problem, but I found out that it
packs a punch.'

'Well I suppose we had better get some rest if we are
going to be working tomorrow.'

As the sun rose people began to emerge from their tents and lorries.
Horses started to whinny for their food and steam rose from kettles
amongst the frying pans. Slowly the mist lifted and the dew evaporated
as the air began to warm.

'It's going to be a very hot day by the looks of it.'

'Is Sarah up yet Robert?'

'I don't think so; I'll bang on her box that should wake her.'

'Trace will you get the feeds and I will do the water!'

'Where are the feeds?'

'In Sarah's box, drop the ramp and they should be at the end, better
get some hay too.'

Robert started to prepare breakfast, Sarah jumped from her
horsebox,—the ladder on the jockey door broke off ages ago.

'Good morning did you all sleep well?' Sarah asked.

'No it was freezing and damp.' Robert grumbled.

'I slept really well I had my gas heater on which kept it lovely
and cosy, I have enough room for two others maybe three if we
squeezed in.'

Robert and the girls almost fell over, as they were not use to such
generous words from Sarah.

'Is there any tea in the pot?' Sarah enquired.

'Yes it has just brewed, have you had a personality change over
night, or have you been replaced by an alien like in the film The
Bodysnatchers?' Al asked.

'No, I have decided that we are here to enjoy ourselves and so there is no time for petty squabbles.' Sarah replied as she poured herself a cuppa.

'Oh I'm glad you have decided.'

'Now Al, Sarah is making an effort, let's be charitable and call a truce, at least until we get home.'

'All right, I will be nice if she is.'

Robert cooked bacon and eggs for breakfast after which they started to prepare for their classes. Sarah was first to compete in her Arab class, Robert tied Prim to the lorry and started to groom her while she munched on a hay net. Al and Trace cleared things away and laid out the saddles and tack as well as their own clothes, which they hung in the lorry to allow the creases to fall out.

'Here's the chalk Robert for her legs, just rub it on and then brush it off until they are white.'

'I do know Sarah I do the same with Lennie, you get yourself ready and I will attend to Prim.'

Al's dressage was not until the afternoon, her time to start was 14.20 and so she had plenty of time to prepare. Sarah put on her usual red outfit with her number, which was 33; her skirt was shorter to prevent a reoccurrence of what happened at a previous show. Prim's feet were cleaned and oiled and her bridle was given a quick polish along with Sarah's boots.

Would competitors for the Arab in hand go to ring two now please.

Sarah trotted Prim up and down to warm her up and then entered the ring, Trace and Al were watching from the ringside. Twenty-three other Arabs entered as well, all of varying heights and colours. Sarah glanced up and down and realised that the competition for first place was going to be of a very high standard. The Arabs were led off and walked in a circle, one or two started to rear up and misbehave, Prim trotted round unperturbed by the antics of others. The judges' steward then asked them all to trot, which most did other then a few who thought that canter was easier, as Sarah began to tire the judge asked the Arabs to walk much to Sarah's relief. The judge called one Arab in after the other in his preferred order of viewing, Prim was somewhere in the middle. As each Arab was called out the judge looked over them stroking and feeling for any bumps and lumps and then they were asked to walk away and trot back passing the judge. Eventually it was Prim's turn, the judge asked how old she was and then checked her over, Sarah walked her away and preyed that nothing would happen on the trot back. Sarah turned round and began to trot back, Prim collected herself up and floated across the ground without a hitch and Sarah returned and saluted the judge and took her place in the line up. Once all the Arabs had been viewed the judge's steward asked them to lead off in a circle, this was the crucial moment when he made his decision on the final order.

'Number 124, please come in, then 28, 34, 56, 178 and 33, the rest of you may leave thank you for attending.' The steward shouted.

Sarah could not believe she had made the final six, they lined up in the order they were called, the judge walked down the line once again lifting the hooves and checked for anything that would alter the placing of the Arab. One of the Arabs lashed out at the judge as he checked its hoof, another was a little cow hocked, once the judge had finished the Arabs were asked to walk off.

'Number 124 please come in and then 33, 34, 28, 178 and 56.'

Sarah was ecstatic at getting a second, but she had to be professional and not show it. The judge gave Sarah her blue rosette, ten pounds winnings and complimented her on Prim's good behaviour and elegant paces. The Arabs led off and exited the ring to a round of applause.

'Well done Sarah that was some competition I didn't think you would be placed.'

'That's nice, Prim is a very well bred Arab you know, mind you even I had my doubts when I saw what the others were like.'

They all returned to the lorry and had some lunch, again prepared by Robert. This time it was chips and ham salad, once they had finished they went for a walk to see what the competition was like and to check out the dressage arena. While they were away the horses had a chat amongst themselves.

'How was it Prim?' Daff enquired.

'Well it was the usual being led around work, there were some nice horses but I did my best and got a blue flower.'

'What do you reckon Lyric shall we do our best or be naughty.'

'Well Prim did her best, so if we misbehave we will be letting her down as well as the mistresses!' Lyric picked up some hay he found.

'I suppose so, that doesn't mean we can't mess about in the warm up though, I mean you have to keep them on their toes.'

'Well if you must Daff, but they have put a lot of work into being here.'

'Whenever I see them they are always eating, I don't see that being a lot of work!' Daff yawned.

The girls returned and Robert started to groom Daff while Al got ready. She put on her cream jodhpurs, black jacket and white stock, Daff had his black dressage saddle and bridle put on with a white square numnah. It was 14.00 and time for Al to warm up, she took Daff to the warm up arena and started to walk him round, she then trotted and cantered on a long rein then she gradually took a contact and started to do some lateral work. Daff started to shake his head from side to side and go behind the vertical to the point that his nose was almost touching his chest. Al tried desperately to push him on but Daff decided a bit of bucking was in order and as Al didn't have her draw-rein he was free to try! The bucking started and then he twisted and bucked and came very close to the fencing. Al tried to gain control but Daff was enjoying himself too much, his bucks became bigger and then he added a few fly kicks as well as a rear. Al managed just to stay on, Daff seemed to know when Al was about to be separated from him and hit the deck and so stopped. Al gathered herself together and got her wind back; Daff was snorting away and chomping on the bit.

'You all right Al, that was quite a tantrum.' Trace was watching from the side of the arena.

'Tell me about it, I just hope he has got it out of his system and doesn't do it in the test.'

Al took a contact and proceeded to warm up, or should I say calm down! Daff began to work properly, once all paces and tricky bits of the test were rehearsed Al returned to the lorry for a last minute brush up and to put her number 45 on.

At 14.20 Al went to the Dressage arena to wait for her slot.

'Number 45 please go in.'

The dressage tests were being held in an indoor arena, spectators were able to watch from seated areas, Sarah, Robert and Trace took their seats. Al entered and walked Daff around he was still a little tense and on his toes as he had never done a test with seated spectators. Al trotted and cantered and Daff slowly relaxed. The judge was seated behind letter C with a steward beside her who completed the dressage score-sheets, the hooter sounded. Al gathered herself together and took a deep breath, she put Daff into working trot and entered at A down the centre line, she went left remembering to get bend but not too much. At E she started her twenty-metre circle left trying not to allow Daff to fall in or have square sides to the circle. When she returned to E she had to do another ten meter circle and change at X and do another ten meter circle to B, the important thing here was not to cross the X too late or early. Between F and A transition to walk and then back to trot was required, so far so good Al then had to begin a twenty metre circle with a transition to canter over X, would Daff buck or canter on the wrong leg Al wondered? Al asked Daff to canter and he did so faultlessly right on X, then canter around the arena to M, between MXK Al had to give and retake the reins without Daff breaking the canter or loosing shape, again he behaved himself. Al started to enjoy things a little, at K trot was required, which Daff did smoothly, next was the difficult part lengthened trot between FXH, Daff either did this or he would run, do nothing or canter. Al sat deeper took a shorter contact and put both legs on evenly, Daff pushed his shoulders forward straightened his front legs, brought his back legs well underneath and lengthened, Al's fixed smile turned into a massive grin. CMB was working trot; this is where the test repeated itself on the other rein. Daff did all that was asked of him without being naughty, he even managed to stand square at the end without swinging his quarters or leaving a hoof dragging.

'Well done Al, he was brilliant, even his lengthening.' Trace gave Daff a mint.

'I know, I could not believe it especially the way he behaved in the warm up.'

'There are another ten to go so we might as well untack and come back.'

Daff was returned to the lorry, untacked and turned back out. They all returned to the dressage arena to watch and wait for the results. There were thirty-five in the class all shapes, breeds and colours, Al was pleased with Daff but the other competitors all looked the part, slim riders on sixteen hand warm bloods. As the last competitor finished Al and the others went to look at the scoreboard, Al was in second place with three results to come.

'I do not believe it; I'm in second place with three to go at least I get a rosette.'

'That's brilliant Al, I told you he was good, proves looks aren't everything!'

'Oi, what do you mean by that?' Al Scowled.

'Only joking, it's been a good day so far, that only leaves me now for the jumping tomorrow.'

The final results were written in and their placing, Al remained second much to the team's delight.

As the sun began to set the horses were fed, hayed and rugged. Robert prepared the evening meal while Sarah, Al and Trace cleaned themselves up.

'Robert have you got anymore hot water, mines gone cold?'

'Coming right up, just waiting for it to boil.'

'What are you cooking Robert?' Al enquired.

'Tomato soup for starters followed by chips, beans and fish fingers and for afters chocolate mousse.'

'Where did you get all that from?'

'I went to the shops earlier.'

'But the kitty is empty'

'I know, Sarah won ten pounds in her class and gave it to me to buy some food.'

'I don't know what we would have done without you Robert.' Trace said.

'Oh so you didn't ask me to come just because of my boyish charms then.'

'What charms.' Sarah quipped.

'Sarah . . .'

'Only kidding, can't anyone take a joke?'

'Yes but we are not use to it from you, here Robert, here is my ten pounds for anything else we need!' Al gave Robert the ten pounds she won in the dressage.

Robert served the soup in mugs, Sarah almost made a comment but just managed to hold it in when Trace glared at her and while this was being drunk, Robert finished off cooking the main course. Daff stood at the fence tossing his head and whinnying.

'What is up with him?'

'Bread, he hasn't forgotten that he had some last night, Robert do we have any bread left?'

'Yes plenty, I will give Daff a few slices before he has the fencing down and joins us!'

'Why does he like bread so much?'

'Don't know, he likes sugared tea and biscuits as well. Once at a show he found a hot dog on the floor and ate it, dog and all. I think my mum is to blame she was always giving him titbits when he was a yearling, she seemed to think he was a dog.'

'I'm surprised he hasn't had colic eating all that kind of rubbish!' Sarah stated.

'Daff isn't stupid he knows what he can and cannot eat.' Al retorted.

'Hey Trace let's light the Tilley's again.'

Trace and Al filled and lit the Tilley's and then sat to eat the main course and dessert. Once they had finished they all helped Robert to clean away the pots and get things ready for the morning.

'Got any thoughts Trace on what you are going to do tomorrow?'

'Try and get clear, that's if Lyric behaves himself and picks his feet up'

'Well Daff and Prim have been good, well almost!'

'Would anyone like to sleep in the box it is warmer than the trailer and the tent?' Sarah asked.

'Well that tent is a bit small and not very warm; you are on, thanks Sarah.'

'If you two are going in the lorry can I have your tent I kept on knocking the pots and pans in the trailer?'

'No problem Robert you can come in the box if you want.'

'Thanks but it would be too cramped and I like my space, besides I do not want to disturb you as I get up earlier to get the breakfast on, besides that what would people think!'

The team retired to their sleeping bags after checking the horses were all right.

> **'Well that's another day over with I wonder when we are going home?' Lyric grumbled.**
>
> **'It's just as well that you did your competition today Daff, I doubt you would manage anything after eating all that bread!'**
>
> **'I have had bread for years and it hasn't slowed me at all.'**
>
> **'What were you playing at, I saw you bucking and rearing, that wasn't very nice you know you almost had her off!' Lyric tutted.**
>
> **'The point is that I didn't throw her, just woke her up a bit, I behaved myself in the class didn't I. I even managed to get a blue flower just like Prim.'**
>
> **'Not the point one of these days you are going to go too far.' Lyric scorned.**
>
> **'Yes, yes. Looks like it is your turn tomorrow let's see if you can get a blue flower or do your usual trick of dropping you hoof and taking some poles down.'**
>
> **'I am going to get a red flower which is better then a blue one.'**

Another day dawned, Robert was already up and making the breakfast and he had the hot water ready for the girls to wash in. Trace fed the horses while Al gave them water and Sarah hayed them. Further down the field a commotion had started.

'What's going on down there Trace?'

'Don't know . . . Yes I do there is a loose horse and they are trying to catch it. If I didn't know better I would think Lennie was here.'

'Well at least they have hold of it even though they are being dragged. Well that's two who now have a lead rope on it. Oh no it is heading this way, quick grab some whips before it ploughs into all our stuff.'

The team grabbed anything they could find to frighten the horse away from their equipment, closer it came, it was at least sixteen hands, by now no-one had hold of it. Dafydd let out a loud neighing sound and the horse slowed down and stopped in front of Daff and stared at him, at least that is what it looked like. Trace and Al hesitantly got hold of the dangling, shredded, lead-ropes; Robert grabbed some bread and fed it to the horse who began to calm down. The owners eventually caught up and couldn't stop thanking Al and Trace for catching their horse. They led their horse away after putting a bridle on it, Al and Trace looked at each other in disbelief, why had the horse stopped when Daff neighed. The girls went back to their breakfast and then went to check the classes and order of competition.

> **'That wasn't a very nice thing you said to that horse Daff!' Prim whickered.**
>
> **'What do you expect; he was heading straight for my bread as well as my mistress.'**
>
> **'You are mad, totally insane you spend most of your time trying to throw her off and then risk life and limb insulting a horse ten times your size!'**
>
> **'What was he going to do, come and bite me; he has to get through this nasty fencing first!'**

The team arrived at the ring to discover that the jumping was being held indoors.

'Oh no Al I didn't realise the jumping was indoors, I have only done outdoor jumping!'

'Just do your best aim to go slow and turn quicker, that's all you have to do.'

'But you know what Lyric is like he only clears things at speed.'

'Calm down he will be fine in fact he will probably jump better, come on your class begins at eleven and you are the tenth in out of twenty-five, lets go and watch we have plenty of time.'

The team went and watched the 2'3" class making the usual comments of—she should have had her leg on-and-she is as stiff as a board-and so it went on. After the team had had their fill they returned to the lorry and prepared Lyric for his class as well calming Trace.

'He's not going to do it you know, he will have the first fence down and then he will refuse the second, if he jumps it he'll knock it down.'

'Trace TRACE—he will do it but if you go in there with a negative attitude he will have a negative attitude, so think positive. Robert did you get any booze? If she can't do it sober she can do it under the influence!'

'Well I did get a bottle of wine for a celebration later.'

'That will do, we will celebrate now!'

Robert fetched the wine and they all had a glass, Trace had two! Trace was not just worried about Lyric not jumping but about letting the team down they had done so well and now it all rested on her shoulders. Lyric was brushed and tacked up in his best boots and numnah and Trace was brushed down and legged up onto Lyric, her boots were given a final polish and she set off to warm up. The others put everything away and raced over to the indoor arena, now was not the time for any advice it was just a case of Trace and Lyric sorting themselves out.

The course looked massive, just as the team got seated Lyric entered the arena and stopped dead the question was—was it lyric or Trace that had stopped? Lyric moved on forward and trotted around the arena having a quick look at the fences Trace never walks the course; it is one of her superstitions and the fact that the fences always look bigger from the ground. Lyric unusually bucked which seem to jolt Trace into taking up the reins and getting into a jump position. The bell went, Trace cantered Lyric and set him up for the first jump which he flew, Trace tried to pull him back off the second but Lyric was having none of it, feet tucked neatly up he jumped the second. The third jump was a double, Trace had to get him back for this otherwise he would be too fast for the second part, Lyric slowed his pace and just managed to clear the second fence. Fence four was a spread which Lyric misjudged slightly as he just clipped the top pole, the pole rolled back and forth and eventually settled in the cups. Fence five was a wall, six and seven uprights, five . . . clear . . . . six clear . . . . seven . . . . clear . . . Trace and Lyric did it they had cleared the first round a round of applause was heard as Trace and Lyric left the arena. The team rushed outside:

'Well done Trace that was brilliant, I have never seen him jump so well, indoor jumping obviously agrees with him.'

'I don't believe he did that, did you see he cleared all the jumps, he was so strong all I could do was sit there, I tried to slow him for the double but I had to give up and just go with him.'

'He was unbelievable, did you stop when you entered or did he?'

'I am afraid it was me the jumps looked massive but he seemed to shrug his shoulders and started off before I told him, are you sure you didn't give him any wine!'

'I suppose because you were a little more relaxed he figured there was nothing to be scared of and just got on with the job.

'There are another fifteen to go so let's go back to the box.'

The team returned to the box and tied Lyric up with some Hay.

**'Hey Lills how did you do, did you manage to keep
your hooves out of the jumps?'**

'Actually I did, apart from one that I rattled, well as you say you have to keep the mistresses on their toes!'

'You have got to go in again haven't you?'

'Yes the next one is where I can go really fast, it is just a question of the mistress staying on top and leaving my mouth alone. She can really pull when she wants to but if I do it her way I will make a mistake.'

'Well make a mistake then we can all go home or we will be here forever.'

'No Daff you have done a class, I have done one when Lyric has done his we can go home, so do you best Lyric.'

'I intend to.'

Would the twelve clear round riders return to the arena
for the 2'6" jump off

'That's you Trace, time to get back on.'

'Do I have to can't you do it?'

'How much wine have you had?'

'Rather a lot this bottle was nearly full.' Robert held up an empty bottle.

'Why didn't anyone stop her, quick get some coffee on.'

'Too late by the time we have made it, the jump off will be over, just get her on Lyric he will look after her.'

Together the team hoisted Trace onto Lyric, Trace had hiccups which started her laughing and worse of all she started to sing.

'Trace shut up you will have everyone looking at us.'

'Wassup, I am relaxed aren't I.'

'Well that is true, are you going to be able to do the jump off?'

'Sure I can, old Lills will look after me won't you my little hairy beast.'

'Just hold on and point him in the right direction, oi wake up.'

'What, I was just having a little rest.'

'Trace wake up and get the job done we are all relying on you.'

Al led Trace and Lyric over to the warm up arena, Trace managed to get Lyric over a few jumps and then it was her turn to do the jump off. Al told Trace several times what the jump off was as to whether it went in only time would tell.

Lyric entered the arena Trace just remained on top. Trace rode Lyric to the top end of the arena where she promptly threw up in the corner; a big groan was heard from the spectators. Trace wiped her mouth on her sleeve, she felt much better after that, she gathered up her reins and the bell went. The jump off was over fences one, three five and seven. Trace pushed Lyric on and got some momentum going, round she went to fence one, inside fence two sharp turn left to fence three, Trace was just a passenger she was too sloshed to slow Lyric up. Lyric realised almost too late that he was not going to make the second part with an almighty stretch he bounced the double instead of one stride as Trace was so relaxed she went with him. A gasp of disbelief echoed through the arena as Lyric practically turned in mid air to leap over the wall. Once he landed he went into overdrive to cut past fence six and to clear fence seven which he did with spectacular ease, all Trace had to do now was stop which she did and promptly fell off luckily it was after the finish. The team went down and scooped Trace up and led Lyric out.

'I would have never believed that if I hadn't seen it.'

'What did I do, I didn't get eliminated did I?' Trace hiccupped.

'No you managed to fall off after you finished, Lyric was unbelievable he bounced a double.'

'Excuse me.' A young man approached the team.

'I wondered if you would like to sell that horse he has great potential and I run a jumping team, I will pay a fare price?'

'No way he is not for sale at any price, sorry.' Trace came to her senses for a moment.

'Well here is my card if you change your mind. I must say I have never seen anyone ride the way you have just done, it is quite unique, good day.'

'Come on lets get Trace back to the box before she starts singing again, we will come back for the results.'

The team led Lyric with Trace back in the saddle, as no one was going to carry her, to the horsebox. Robert got some coffee going as well as preparing some sandwiches. Lyric was untacked and turned back out; all the horses were given a feed as a reward for their efforts.

'How did you do Lills?' Daff whinnied.

'Very well I think, the mistress managed to stay on she was like a sack of spuds but at least she left me alone to get on with the job. You should have seen the bounce I did it was meant to be a stride in between.'

'Let me guess you were going too fast.'

'Only a little but I made it and the turns were brilliant.'

'I get the idea Lills hopefully we can go home now.'

The team, except Trace who was laying down in the horsebox, returned to get the results. Out of twelve Trace and Lyric came first, two seconds faster then second place, Al stood in for Trace explaining that she was unwell, needless to say she didn't do the lap of honour. The team ran cheering back to the box, they still had to wait for the overall results and the possibility of winning £300.00 pounds which was not really possible as they would have to get three firsts, they only had one and two seconds.

After eating the sandwiches and clearing away the team started to load everything onto the vehicles.

'Al are you going to drive Tracey's Land Rover as she is going to be well over the drink drive limit?' Sarah enquired.

'I certainly am, it would be best if Robert goes with you and Trace with me she can spread out on the back seat.'

Robert scowled at Al as he did not like the idea of travelling for over an hour with Sarah

Would all teams please return to the indoor arena for the overall results.

The team except Trace went to the indoor school with their rosettes; Robert took Trace's place and stood in the arena.

In third place with one hundred pounds is the Byron team who had one third and two fourths. Second Place and two hundred pounds goes to the Hookahs team with two seconds and a first. First place with three hundred pounds is the Kings team with two firsts and a second, well done to you all.

The team had taken second and two hundred pounds, they could not believe it. They were on cloud nine and so returned to the horsebox to tell Trace who was still asleep.

'Al I did not know we had the name Hookahs when did that happen?'

'Oh it was just something I thought up; after all we needed a name.'

The team loaded the horses; amazingly Daff went in with no problem at all which almost made Al feint as she was all prepared with her lunge rein and gloves. Sarah led the way as the team drove home.

They journey back was without any problems apart from the mandatory traffic jam every so often. As the lorry and trailer arrived in the yard the horses started to whinny to each other. Those in the field rushed to the fence and watched with interest as to who the 'new arrivals' were when they saw Daff, Lyric and Prim they all walked off in disgust.

'Well how did you do?' asked Mike

'We did brilliantly, two hundred pounds, once we have taken out the food and fuel costs we should have a fair bit left for the yard, anything happen while we were away?'

'No all has been quiet, someone turned up wanting to bring their horse here, I told them to come back when you were here.'

The horses were unloaded and turned out; the occasional scuffle broke out amongst the horses as they sorted out the pecking order. Lennie thought he could be the new boss as Daff had 'gone' but Daff soon put him back in his place. The girls put all the equipment away except the things like numnah's and boots that needed to be cleaned, even Trace managed to sort her things out albeit slower then the others. It was not long before the horses were brought in.

'It's nice to be back home I hope we don't have do that too often.' Lyric sighed.

'Well if you had messed up the jumping they would not think about taking us away again, the odd day is acceptable but not overnight.' Daff scorned.

'If that is so then why didn't you carry on with your tantrums in your test then?'

'Because I could not let that Arab over there get a better flower than me, I was making a point.'

'In your dreams Daff, you are lucky if you get a pink one, I usually get a red flower which you very rarely, if ever get and it shows how good I am as my mistress

has a big box to take me in and you have to share!'
Prim snorted.

'She has to have a big box to carry your big head in.'
Daff retorted sarcastically.

FROM THE AUTHOR

Thank you for purchasing The Yard. I have wanted to be an illustrator and author ever since I can remember. I started drawing from the moment I could hold a pencil and yes all the illustrations are done by me without 'professional training'. I never knew what I would illustrate or write until I became the owner of a nine month old colt called Dafydd, his grumpy attitude and ability to cause trouble started the creation of Hookahs Horses cartoons and ultimately the writing of The Yard. Dafydd had the ability to really irritate me; almost breaking my resilience to keep him and to carry on training him, may be one day I will write the true story!

I was born in 1967 in Perivale, Middlesex, London, my father was a manager of an engineering company and mother was a 'stay at home' mum. I had a state school education and left at nineteen doing different jobs. I really wanted to publish my work unfortunately I just could not get a publisher interested. So I self-published in the nineties and failed, so I became a Gardener; which I still do today while continuing to write and illustrate.

Dafydd reached 14.2hh and I trained him right from being led, to lunging, to backing, to hacking and we competed in many disciplines not to any high level, just local shows. Sometimes he would be brilliant and other times a total embarrassment but I was as determined to succeed as he was to cause trouble and so we remained together for 27 years.

As Dafydd aged he became more accepting of things and we built a bond that only death could break. He excelled at dressage and he could really jump but only when he was in the right mood. He developed Cushing's; which in his twenties became a real problem leading to laminitis and hoof abscesses, twice he almost lost his life but his tenacity as well as mine kept him going. He also had arthritis which became really bad. Eventually even the painkillers could not keep the pain away and so I had to make the worse decision that any owner has to make and have him put to sleep. I now have Mistabit who is a distant relation to Dafydd, I got him in late 2007 as Dafydd was getting on and often lame. I searched and tried horses; then came across Misty and bought him after looking at two photographs received on my mobile. He was a bit of a mess but he has turned into a magnificent horse who has not put a hoof wrong and who makes the loss of Dafydd easier.

I hope you have enjoyed this book . . . . Book two is on its way . . . . hopefully followed by book three . . . . .